North Shore Spirits
of Massachusetts

Christopher Forest

Photographs by Melissa R. Forest

4880 Lower Valley Road, Atglen, Pennsylvania 19310

All the photos are by Melissa Brown Forest, except for:
Cover photo: Insane Asylum © Linda MacPhail. Fort Sewell on the coast of Marblehead, Massachusetts © Paula Stephens. Flying Witch Silhouette © Tatyana Okhitina. Photos courtesy BigStockPhotos.com.

Disclaimer The purpose of this book is to share stories regarding the paranormal experiences people have encountered throughout history in the North Shore of Massachusetts. They are meant to entertain; however, we do not suggest that they are necessarily proof of the supernatural...just evidence that we have gathered from multiple sources that describe fascinatingly and often unexplainable stories.

Other Schiffer Books by Christopher Forest
Boston's Haunted History, 978-0-7643-2874-9, $12.95

Schiffer Books are available at special discounts for bulk purchases for sales promotions or premiums. Special editions, including personalized covers, corporate imprints, and excerpts can be created in large quantities for special needs. For more information contact the publisher:

Schiffer Publishing Ltd.
4880 Lower Valley Road
Atglen, PA 19310
Phone: (610) 593-1777; Fax: (610) 593-2002
E-mail: Info@schifferbooks.com

For the largest selection of fine reference books on this and related subjects, please visit our web site at: **www.schifferbooks.com** We are always looking for people to write books on new and related subjects. If you have an idea for a book please contact us at the above address.

This book may be purchased from the publisher. Include $5.00 for shipping. Please try your bookstore first. You may write for a free catalog.

In Europe, Schiffer books are distributed by
Bushwood Books
6 Marksbury Ave.
Kew Gardens
Surrey TW9 4JF England
Phone: 44 (0) 20 8392 8585; Fax: 44 (0) 20 8392 9876
E-mail: info@bushwoodbooks.co.uk
Website: www.bushwoodbooks.co.uk

Designed by Stephanie Daugherty
Type set in a Theme for murder/Rosemary Roman/NewBskvll BT/NewsGoth BT
ISBN: 978-0-7643-3291-3
Printed in the United States of America

Dedication

*T*his book is lovingly dedicated to my wonderful wife, and photographer, Melissa. I am not only fortunate to have her as a wife, but she willingly accompanied me on many of my ghostly adventures. The book is also dedicated to our daughter, Brighid, who often joined us on our travels, as well as our son, Christopher,  who unbeknownst to him, also took several voyages with us...before he was even born!

Acknowledgments

A lot of the work that went into this book was the research conducted by countless people over the course of many years. I thank all of the people involved in creating the resources listed at the end of this book for their tireless efforts. Without them, this book could never have been completed.

I would also like to thank several individuals whose emails and suggestions helped me learn more about the various stories in this book. They include:

❖ "Emmie" — a former tour guide at the House of Seven Gables for her in depth information about the ghosts of the gables.

❖ Shannah Hiatt — an employee at David's Tavern, whose email explained many details regarding the possible haunts at the Garrison Inn and David's Tavern.

❖ Elizabeth Brewin — the former marketer at the Lyceum Restaurant who manages functions at the restaurant. Her email shed a lot of light on the incidents in the restaurant.

❖ Nicholas Smith — He runs Crypto Paranormal Investigations. His email provided helpful information about the work that was done at Fort Sewall and reasons why it might be considered haunted.

❖ Martin Fucio — He works for the National Park Service, and provided some valuable information about the Salem Custom House via email.

❖ Richard Trask — He works for the Danvers Archival Center. He is the resident expert on Danvers and his information was particularly helpful regarding the town library.

Special thanks goes to my wife, Melissa, who took the pictures for this book and followed me every step of the way. And, major kudos go to Jennifer Marie Savage, my gracious editor who has helped keep me on track, and Dinah Roseberry, who helped make this book possible. THANK YOU SO MUCH!

Contents

Contents

Introduction

The stories contained in this book are a composite of many tales told throughout the years. They attempt to capture a glimpse of the supernatural occurrences that might have happened in the North Shore of Massachusetts over the past three centuries. Some of the stories have long been told, while others are more recent. Some have a lengthy story *behind* the story while some have become more of a contemporary urban legend. Most of the stories are based on fact and lore, while a few might be more of a fantastic fabrication.

This book attempts to examine many of those supernatural stories by providing information describing the paranormal nature of the tales and, in some cases, providing evidence that refutes some of the supernatural claims. But whatever the cause behind the story, this book is a unique blend of the paranormal tales that encompass the North Shore region.

Many of the places mentioned here still exist. Yet, some have vanished into history and others may no longer have the access that they once enjoyed. Places that were once open to the public are now businesses or private buildings. Some of the islands featured here no longer allow visitors, and the cemeteries have strict visiting rules.

Ghost enthusiasts are a fun group. However, we ask that if you decide to learn more about these haunts for yourself, that you respect the privacy of those places that have now turned into businesses, residences, or private property, as well respect the rules of the islands and cemeteries that dot the North Shore.

Most importantly, though, as you read this, enjoy the history of Massachusetts's friendly—*and haunted*—North Shore.

Happy hunting.

Part One:
Salem

The Witch Town

Salem. The name itself conjures up a myriad of thoughts. Nathaniel Hawthorne. The China Trade. And of course, the Salem Witch Trials.

While Salem has a special legacy all its own, in contemporary times, it has staked its reputation on being "The Witch City." While the current Salem indeed played a pivotal role in the witch trials, much of the history surrounding the seventeenth century persecution of supposed witches actually took place in towns no longer within Salem City's limits.

Despite this fact, Salem was—and *is* still—considered the supernatural capital of America. Every fall, thousands of people make a pilgrimage to the haunted city. In turn, the city makes way for an influx of people who wish to be scared as well as learn the truth behind all the "witch" stories found in here. Museums, tours, and bookstores teem with history from the day. But, at the same time, Salem also tries to have a little fun, hosting museums and stores that look a little bit like Hollywood haunted houses.

Salem is definitely a site to behold because as Halloween approaches visitors come to frolic in the city. However, many often fail to see that Salem's supernatural legacy has actually existed for quite some time. Come and check out these stories to see why Salem really IS America's haunt land.

1

The Scourge of Salem

The Salem Witch Trials

The History

Seventeenth century New England was a superstitious place. For nearly a century, people had explored the shores of New England in search of fertile soil, plow-able land, and resources. When exploring turned to settling, New England became a booming center of the English colonies.

However, as New England became established, a strict Puritan idea began to blossom throughout the region. The idea of creating a colony highlighted by religious freedom yet mixed with strict morals gained a firm grasp on the land. Nowhere else was this evident than in the coastal towns of Massachusetts, where the Puritan law had been firmly entrenched.

The Puritan morals sometimes clashed with local residents. Anyone who preached a contradictory message was often asked to leave the colony. Those who did not risked death. Under such pretenses, the Puritan code existed for decades. Some of their laws still exist in the state until this day.

While a colony designed to affirm religious beliefs helped maintain peace and order, it created a society that had a superstitious regard to anything it could not understand. Sudden changes in weather, people misbehaving, animals acting contrary to their typical nature...were all thought to have hidden, sometimes deeper meanings.

By the time the 1690s rolled around, New Englanders held such a high regard for their religion that they often misinterpreted events that occurred in their region. Unfortunately, for many people,

This sign marks the vicinity of the Salem Village Meeting House. This was the location of the initial Salem Witchcraft interrogations.

those misinterpretations eventually lead to "witch fever" — a fervent belief that witches were wreaking havoc throughout the colony. For centuries, the idea that witches were inherently tied to evil and could cause trouble for their victims was alive and well in Europe. Witch hunts, witch trials, and witch burnings had been a common phenomenon. And the idea that witches could bewitch others was a real fear to the people in Europe.

However, by the end of the seventeenth century, scientific reasoning had begun to surface in Europe. As this revolution spread, the danger of witches became slightly muted when science began to

Above: This is the foundation of the actual Parris household. It was in this house that the Salem Witch hysteria first began. *Below:* This sign marks the vicinity of the parish where the Salem Witchcraft Trials occurred and eventually ended.

explain some of the unusual phenomenon that had once been relegated to witches. A sudden snow squall on a sunny day... Well, that could be explained as an unusual cold front blowing through. A cow stops giving milk... It might have some type of blockage that can be treated.

While the revolution was occurring in Europe, it had not quite emigrated to America, where the ways of religion and superstition still blended to create an atmosphere of belief—*and fear*—in witchcraft.

In the year 1692, this religious fervor reached a high point in the city of Salem, Massachusetts. And, a series of events unfolded that led to the infamous Salem Witch Trials that have confounded historians for centuries. Those events are rooted not in paranormal activity — as some people believe to this day — but in firmly entrenched, and archaic, beliefs. And so the story goes...

Salem Village was a hot bed of activity in the 1690s. Political factions had divided the small village into two different camps. The Village was growing at odds with the larger Salem Town and the arrival of a new minister named Samuel Parris sparked a renewed Puritanical vigor in the town.

Ironically, the witchcraft problems within the town surfaced first in the Parris household. Here, Reverend Parris's daughter Betty and niece Abigail Williams, who was living at the Parris house, began behaving oddly. At times, the girls would stop speaking. Other times, the girls would act as if they had been pinched by invisible agents. And, sometimes, they would thrash their limbs wildly. Instead of diminishing over time with a typical ailment, the affliction spread to other girls.

Members of the village began to compare their affliction with one that affected children in Boston a few years earlier. There, the children had acted in a similar fashion. A witch had been considered the source of the problem. Believing that such a dilemma was occurring in their village, townsfolk decided to act. They had the local doctor, thought to be William Griggs, examine the girls. When he could not find the source of their problem, the doctor suggested that the girls were indeed bewitched.

The girls were tested, examined, and intensely coerced to name the source of the bewitching. Over time, as a result of the pressure, the girls named three people as their bewitchers — Tituba, Parris's slave (who possibly taught the girls ways to predict the future, which would have been considered a sinful act at the time), and Sarah Good and Sarah Osburn, neither of whom had the best reputation in the village.

The women were eventually arrested and put on trial. The girls would testify to the accused witch's guilt in front of many townsfolk. And, soon, a formal witch "hunt" occurred. The girls continued to name other potential witches, often suffering from fits whenever they were near the accused. Those who admitted to being witches were allowed to live, but those who did not admit to the charges were eventually hanged (or in one instance, when Giles Corey refused to say anything about his charge, pressed to death).

For several months, the village and the town of Salem, as well as more than twenty other towns, were caught up in a witch frenzy. The village girls were often taken to other towns to root out witches. At the trials' end, twenty people were killed; five died in jail, and about 160 people were arrested.

Several events brought about the end of the trials. Residents in surrounding towns began to question the motives of those who accused people of being witches. Some of the Puritan leaders in Boston, particularly Cotton Mather, called into question the use of spectral evidence (when a witch came to a person in a dream or as a vision) as a way to identify a witch. And, when the wife of Massachusetts's governor, William Phips, was targeted as a witch, the trials were brought to an abrupt halt.

The Mystery

The brief description above only summarizes the events of the day. Books are dedicated to the subject — and actual transcripts still exist from the time — to give us a better understanding of the entire events as they unfolded. They are definitely worth reading.

However, the witch trials have puzzled and awed people for years. Some people still believe that supernatural means were involved in the trial. However, it's important to note that there is no evidence to support that anything supernatural was afflicting the girls or the village (although, there is an unusual note from one of the trials that suggests some strange force visited the meetinghouse while an accused witch was on the stand, as a gust of wind blew open a door, rattled papers, blew out candles, and then quickly disappeared). So, if you do visit Salem and the surrounding areas, be aware that the 1690s "witches" are not witches at all...even though modern witches do claim Salem as their home.

The reasons behind the trial actually do remain a mystery, because no one is too sure how the witch-hunt unfolded so quickly and harshly. Why the girls behaved the way they did — and why the people of Salem accepted their story — remains a mystery that might forever be unsolved. However, there are four interesting possibilities that historians have considered as the main cause:

❖ **Political problems**: The village had been in a bit of political turmoil during the years before the witch trials. Different groups in the town had bickered over land boundaries, church membership, and other problems. In some respects, two "factions" had been created and, as the trials played out, members of one faction, the ones who sided with the powerful families in town, were the accusers, and members of the other faction were often the accused.

❖ **Fear of Native Americans**: King Phillip's War ended about sixteen years before the witch trials began. The long-fought war between the Native Americans and colonists ended in devastation for both sides — particularly the Native Americans. Nearly every town in New England had been affected by the war. A fear of the Native American friendship with the French settlements in Canada, a misunderstanding of the Native American's religion, which Puritans considered a stark contrast to their own, and the idea that Native American's might seek retribution for the war fueled fears of anything unknown… like witches.

❖ **Ergot**: This disease, caused by tainted wheat, often caused convulsions and in some cases hallucinations in people who ingested the wheat. While some studies from the time suggest that the people in Salem Village were not exposed to such wheat, the description of the girls' behavior is similar to those who had been exposed to it.

❖ **Mass delusion**: Many historians believe (and some studies confirm) that the girls in question became part of a mass delusion. When they engaged in the fortune telling, violating the Puritan rules of the time, the girls began to worry about repercussions and soon acted peculiarly. When pressed about the behavior, the girls didn't know how to respond. Realizing that townsfolk thought they were bewitched, the girls replied that they were, and eventually may have begun believing their own stories.

And, so it happened. The Salem Witch Trials remain a mysterious, unfortunate chapter in American history. It's a sad legacy that Salem has to endure, but it was hardly caused by the supernatural. Yet, this association with witches has made Salem a supernatural center in the United States. Ghost enthusiasts, psychics, real witches, and perhaps even a few ghosts themselves, have slowly but surely built Salem into America's most haunted homeland.

2

The House of Several Ghosts

The Spirits of Seven Gables

The History

*I*t's an icon in American literature—a book that has been well known for generations, a literary work that you just might have read with delight, or perhaps not, in high school. It is the *House of Seven Gables*.

Nathaniel Hawthorne's American classic has satisfied readers for decades. And, for nearly half that time, the house that some say played prominently in the story — the Turner-Ingersoll Mansion — has become an American jewel of its own. Located along the Salem seashore, the Turner-Ingersoll Mansion welcomes many visitors each year who hope to step foot into the literary past.

The mansion, built in 1668, is believed to be the oldest wooden mansion still in existence in New England. It became part of American lore when it was included in Hawthorne's famous tome. It's worth noting that Hawthorne said that he had not truly envisioned the mansion as the house in his story... however, he does describe a house that is remarkably similar in appearance to this one, which he would have been familiar with given that he was resident of Salem. Because of its association with the book, you don't hear too many people say, "Hey, let's go visit the Turner-Ingersoll Mansion." Most refer to it as the *House of Seven Gables*.

The Turner Ingersoll Mansion is better known as the House of Seven Gables. Made famous by Nathaniel Hawthorne, it's believed to be the home of several ghosts...perhaps even the ghost of Hawthorne himself.

In 1908, Caroline Emmerton, a noted philanthropist, purchased the home and restored it over a two-year period. Her dream was to open the house to the public and use the proceeds to fund programs for people in need. In the process, the house has become a remarkable piece of history, showcasing some of its original seventeenth and eighteenth century charm, as well as the famous "secret staircase" that leads people to the attic.

The *House of Seven Gables* site, however, is more than just the mansion. It's a small compound, consisting of various houses resting on the site. Several other houses were moved and restored at the site, making the spot actually an historic district. And, those houses have unique histories of their own. Chronologically speaking, the property also includes:

❖ **The Retire Becket House**: Dating to 1655, it's named for the Beckets, a family of shipbuilders who helped establish the Salem shipping trade in Japan. The house was moved to the site in 1924.

❖ **The Hooper-Hathaway House**: Built in 1682, it's named for two families who lived in the house. Benjamin Hathaway, a cordwainer who lived there, built the house. Over time, it passed through a couple of families, arriving in the hands of the Hathaway family in 1864. The Hathaways were local bakers and their home was often nicknamed "The Old Bakery" before it was threatened with demolition in 1911. Emmerton rescued the home and added it to the collection.

❖ **The Nathaniel Hawthorne Birthplace**: Built around 1750, it was originally believed to be the home of a mariner named Joshua Pickman. He may have lived in the house until Hawthorne's grandfather purchased it in 1772. Hawthorne was born there July 4, 1804. The house was moved to the site of the Seven Gables in 1958.

❖ **The Phippen House**: Built around 1782, the three-story house belonged to Joshua Phippen in the late 1700s. Phippen was a cooper in Salem. The house is currently closed to visitors.

❖ **The Counting House:** Dating back to the 1830s, this Counting house is typical of the time and was a place where captains would have done much of their business. Counting houses were important in Salem during the height of the China Trade.

In addition to the houses, the grounds are home to several old trees and two remarkable gardens. The property also contains 2,000 artifacts dating to the different time periods each house reflects.

The Seven Gables property has enchanted visitors for years. Emmerton's dream continues to be realized, as proceeds from the property are used to help fund the Settlement House across the street. The house provides programs for school-age children in the community throughout the year.

The Mystery

The *House of Seven Gables* is rich in tradition and history for the average visitor to share. However, there is a bit of history that occasionally appears that the typical visitor might not always be able to experience. For, according to some sources, the *House of Seven Gables* may also be the "House of Several Ghosts."

Various stories are told about the ghosts that inhabit the compound. Many of them involve the dining room of the Turner-Ingersoll Mansion. Some people believe that the ghost of a woman, perhaps one time inhabitant Susan Ingersoll, haunts this room.

People who have visited the house claim that the attic is also haunted. While people might not always see a ghost in this room, visitors claim to *feel* a strange presence there—a presence often associated with feeling of gloom or sadness.

Some visitors who have taken pictures of the building report seeing a shadowy figure appear in the windows of the gables. This isn't your ordinary tourist peering out of a window, though. The figure is believed to be a woman who peers out the window, gazing off in the distance. The woman can be found in different windows, depending on the pictures that are taken of the grounds (none are permitted inside, so most photographs taken of the structure come from the back sidewalk section). At least once, a photographer noted that someone was tapping the window during a picture-taking session. Even more interesting, it was *after* the Gables had closed for the day and no one was working in that section of the house. Perhaps this was the ghost trying to get someone's attention.

Other people suggest that the most haunted building on site is the Nathaniel Hawthorne Birthplace. Visitors to this site have mentioned that they *felt* a presence in the building when they entered. Some visitors have claimed to see the ghost of a boy who resides there. Exactly who the boy is remains unknown. However, in an article found on the Internet, "The Ghosts of Seven Gables," the author suggests that the ghost might be the wandering spirit of Nathaniel Hawthorne when he was a young lad. The reason his youthful spirit might remain in the house, despite the fact that he grew up to be an adult, was that he learned of his father's death at sea while he was living at the house as a young boy. Because some ghost hunters believe that great tragedy allows ghosts to linger in an area, such a misfortune

might explain why Hawthorne's ghost, manifesting itself as a lad, permeates the house.

One former tour guide of the Gables did mention a bit about the ghostly legacy of the Gables. "Emmie," as she preferred to be called, spent time giving tours of the mansion and worked in the Nathaniel Hawthorne Birthplace. While she was aware of the stories involving the mansion — and did acknowledge that the dining room was believed to be haunted — she never experienced anything out of the ordinary.

However, Emmie did note that the Hawthorne Birthplace site seemed to have something special happening inside it.

"I never saw anything there," Emmie explains. "However, I did sense a presence in the Birthplace on some occasions. From time to time the presence was particularly strong."

Emmie mentions that the presence rarely manifested itself during the operational hours. Usually, it occurred toward the end of the workday, when most visitors had left, or were leaving. Then, it would make itself known.

"I could often hear footsteps on the floor above me," Emmie said. It was always after all workers had left the building and no one was in the floor above her. When asked if she thought the ghost might be that of a young boy, Emmie concedes that she really was not sure, but adds, "It always seemed like an adult to me."

So what is happening in the old *House of Seven Gables*? No one is quite sure. However, it seems entirely possible that some of the old ghosts of Salem may have found a new home in one of America's most famous landmarks. Nathaniel Hawthorne would be proud.

Nathaniel Hawthorne's Ghost Legacy

Often, places that are considered to have a high degree of paranormal activity are called "hot spots;" the Bermuda Triangle, haunted houses, even Salem are considered to be hot spots.

However, if a person could be a "hot spot," there would certainly be no finer example than Nathaniel Hawthorne. When it comes to ghostly occurrences, Hawthorne has no comparison. Sure, you might have been haunted by Hawthorne's writing in high school, having to read a heavy dose of *The Scarlet Letter*, *The House of Seven* Gables, and *Young Goodman Brown* in sophomore English class. However, his haunting legacy might extend beyond these stories. There are no fewer than nine spooky sites (or in one case, situation) that are associated with Salem's native son:

❖ **Curse of Giles Corey (Salem)**: It's unknown if Hawthorne ever saw the ghost of Giles Corey. However, he is known for having mentioned the Curse of Giles Corey, suggesting, like others, that Giles Corey's ghost seems to appear anytime a huge tragedy faces the town of Salem.

❖ **The Hawthorne Hotel (Salem)**: This well-known Salem hotel is named for Salem's favorite literary son. At least one spirit is thought to haunt the site. It often manifests itself in the hotel's restaurant. Whether or not it likes the food is unknown, but supposedly the ghost does like to steer the ship's wheel that hangs on the wall.

❖ **The Lyceum (Salem)**: Now a restaurant, the old Lyceum Hall was a prominent place for lectures in the nineteenth century. It was run by the Salem Lyceum Society, of which Hawthorne was secretary and as such helped arrange speakers. The hall became a restaurant, which is said to be the home of witchcraft victim Bridget Bishop's ghost.

❖ **The Old Burial Point Cemetery (Salem)**: Fond of wandering through cemeteries, Hawthorne visited this cemetery, which some people claim is haunted. One of the gravestones was the inspiration for one of his characters, Dr. Swinnerton.

❖ **Salem Custom House (Salem)**: Hawthorne worked here at one point in time as he prepared to make his mark as an author. At least one ghost is believed to haunt it.

❖ **Danvers State Hospital (Danvers)**: At one time, this property belonged to Hawthorne's ancestor (Jonathan Hathorne) who was a judge in the Salem Witch Trials. Nathaniel actually changed the spelling of his name, adding a "w," because of his disdain being associated with a Witch Trial participant. The former state hospital, now called Hawthorne Hill, was considered one of the most haunted sites in the country following the close of the hospital. Most of the hospital has been demolished to make way for private homes—and it appears the ghosts may have finally left. Since the new

houses have been built, there have been no publicized sightings of ghosts.

❖ **The original Boston Athenaeum (Boston)**: This large library was a frequent stop for Hawthorne. However, it's also the home of a ghost (who may have moved to the current location of the Athenaeum) named Reverend Harris. The first person to mention seeing this ghost was none other than Nathaniel Hawthorne. He claimed to have seen—and *spent time with*—the Reverend's ghost over the course of several days. He later wrote a short story about the ghost.

❖ **King's Chapel Cemetery (Boston)**: Hawthorne loved to roam cemeteries. This particular cemetery was a favorite. He may have come up with the idea for part of *The Scarlet Letter* when, while roaming this cemetery, he found a gravesite with a large letter "A" on it (the person who it belonged to had nothing to do with the theme found in Hawthorne's story). Some people believe that this cemetery may be home to Captain Kidd's ghost, which could be conjured up under the right conditions. Of course, no one now knows what those conditions are.

❖ **The Omni Parker Hotel (Boston)**: Hawthorne frequently visited this famous hotel during trips to Boston. Often, he met with other authors to discuss topics of the day. The hotel has since been reportedly haunted by various ghosts, including author Charles Dickens, whom Hawthorne met with when the British author was in Boston.

Author's Note: You can find out more about the Boston sites listed here in my first book, *Boston's Haunted History*.

3

Salem's Haunted Restaurant

The Lyceum on Church Street

The History

The first embers of the fire that would become the Salem Witch Trials sparked in the town of Danvers. There, a young lady named Bridget Bishop was slowly earning a reputation that eventually led others to doubt her sincerity.

Bridget Bishop was known as a wild spirit in the local town. The owner of two houses in the area — one in Salem Village (Danvers) and one in Salem Town (Salem) — she was considered a mysterious woman.

Bridget Bishop was also known as the local party girl of her day. Although she lived in the Danvers house with her husband (the house still stands today), Bishop frequently partied with other gentlemen as well, inviting them to her house and keeping them there until late hours. Often the men imbibed alcohol and took part in a various kinds of revelries, including card games.

Because of such behavior went against the Puritanical grain of the community, many villagers and townsfolk cast a wary eye in Bishop's direction. So, when her name was raised as one of the possible witches that inhabited the town, most people openly believed the claim. It was not the first time Bishop had been accused of being a witch. In fact, it seemed a logical explanation for Bishop's behavior.

Bishop was arrested April 18, 1692 and brought to the Ingersoll Ordinary for questioning. There, Bishop was formally accused of witchcraft.

The Lyceum Restaurant is located on the former site of Bridget Bishop's apple orchard. The ghost of this accused witch is thought to haunt the restaurant.

"I know not what a witch is," Bishop replied.

The magistrates were not convinced and placed Bishop on trial June 2. As typically occurred during the proceedings, several forms of evidence was brought forth regarding Bishop's guilt. Most of the evidence was spectral, although residents John and William Bly reportedly found dolls filled with pins located in the walls of her Salem home. Surely, they thought, this was proof enough of her witchcraft.

Despite proclaiming her innocence, Bishop was indeed found guilty and hanged nine days later, becoming the first official victim of the trials.

However, that might not have been the end of Bridget Bishop. Many people claim that her lingering spirit inhabits the restaurant known as *The Lyceum*, which is located on the property she once owned.

The Lyceum Restaurant, located around the corner from the Peabody Essex Museum, has been open as a restaurant since 1989. Catering to a variety of tastes, the restaurant is a fine establishment that serves memorable meals in a quaint atmosphere.

The Lyceum opened in a former lecture hall that once dominated the Salem landscape. Several famous people lectured there, including Ralph Waldo Emerson, Frederick Douglass, and Henry David Thoreau. Alexander Graham Bell gave his first public demonstration of the phone at the hall. Nathaniel Hawthorne served as secretary of the institution, arranging speakers to talk to the group members. The eloquent structure, completed with an old-fashioned safe and large hearth, speaks to a learned time in American history.

The Lyceum itself was a society dedicated to sharing knowledge and engaging in public debate. Formed in 1830, the group originally met in the Universalist Meeting House and then the town hall before the hall was constructed and opened in January 1831. The hall was built on property purchased from local resident Sarah Orne and the building cost a whopping $3,036.76. The Lyceum sponsored lectures every Tuesday night, open to the public, charging $1 for men and seventy-five cents for women. Ironically, no debates were ever held at the Lyceum, but more than 1,000 lectures were given there.

The Mystery

The Lyceum is not just one of the finest restaurants and historical sites in Salem—it's believed to be home to the ghost of Bridget Bishop. Throughout the history of the Salem restaurant, the ghost has been spotted in the restaurant and mysterious things have happened to people who visited.

The most popular sighting occurs on the main staircase leading to the second floor of the restaurant. There, many people have claimed to see the ghost of a woman descending the staircase. The ghost lasts only momentarily...*and then disappears*. Witnesses who have seen her distinctly claim that she is dressed in old fashioned garbed, suggesting that she indeed is a ghost from the seventeenth century.

The second level of the restaurant, which serves as a function hall, appears to be particularly haunted. But, while the ghost of Bridget Bishop is seen occasionally on the staircase, it makes itself known in other, stranger ways. Several television shows have attempted to film at the restaurant, including Food TV. As is often the case in settings where there's (alleged) supernatural activity, the crews often experienced electrical trouble with cameras, lights, and other equipment...that could not be explained. The same can be said for photographers who attempted to take pictures on the second level. Cameras often failed to work, or, when they did, fail to take pictures.

According to an email from Elizabeth Brewin, an event manager and former marketer at the Lyceum Restaurant, the second floor is the source of most of the ghost stories.

"The thing that always gets me is the photography problem (on the second floor)," Brewin wrote.

Although Brewin has never had a first-hand encounter with any ghosts, many photographers have come to the building to photograph functions or the haunted spots at the restaurant. Often, the photographers who come for functions have no problem—but the minute someone comes to take pictures of the restaurant because it might be haunted, problems typically occur. Brewin mentioned one incident in particular: a photographer who was taking pictures of haunted sites in the region arrived at the restaurant. The photographer took pictures of the Lyceum and other places on one roll of film. All of the photographs of the other places turned out fine, but each one of the Lyceum turned out fuzzy and difficult to see.

The Atlantic Paranormal Society, or TAPS, as members of the "Ghost Hunters" television show, attempted to visit the site. Although they found no paranormal activity during their visit, they did record the cash register printing a receipt that said "Good Morning" on its own. According to workers, the cash register never acts this way.

Bridget's ghost may not be relegated to manifestations and strange electrical problems. Many people report the strange scent of apples floating in the restaurant air, with no apparent reason. There is no apple pie cooking in the kitchen and no apple cider being served...in fact, the menu typically lacks apple recipes. However, the apples are often distinct and powerful, suggesting that the ghost of Bridget Bishop may be revisiting her old apple orchard and picking the ripest fruit from her trees.

Exactly who or what might be the source of these strange phenomenon remain unknown. Yet, enough people have experienced such encounters at the Lyceum that people sometimes consider it one of the most haunted buildings on the North Shore.

4

Salem's Haunted Hotel

The Hawthorne Hotel

The History

In the mid 1700s, Salem became a port city of some prominence in the world. Ships leaving the city would circumnavigate the globe looking for wares to sell in America. After journeys that could take years to culminate, ships would return with fabulous bounties.

Captains and crew alike not only returned with treasures, but grandiose stories to share. By the latter half of the eighteenth century, it became obvious to these seafaring folk that their brotherhood could benefit from organizing a society where they could gather to meet and share stories.

In 1766, the sailors in town founded the Maritime Society. In a small building in the center of town, they could enjoy the camaraderie of each other while waiting for the next trip out to sea. The Maritime Society became a popular group with the seafaring community.

However, as times changed and Salem's port became overshadowed by other Atlantic ports, new needs occurred in town. This included a need for a hotel to cater to visitors who traveled into the city. Politicians and city elders gathered to choose the right spot and selected the site of the Maritime Society as the place to build the hotel.

By that time, the society's building was older. The members of the society made a deal with the hotel owners: they would give them their land in exchange for a meeting place that would be added to the hotel.

In time, the Hawthorne Hotel sprung up on the site of the old Maritime Society, complete with a meeting place at the penthouse

★ NATHANIEL ★
HAWTHORNE
★ 1804 — 1864 ★

level for the sailor's organization. Six stories high, it was—and still is—the largest building in town and, as with all buildings, it has its share of grandiose tales.

The Mystery

Just the name of the building — Hawthorne Hotel — might conjure up ghostly images. After all, Nathaniel Hawthorne spent time there writing ghostly tales of the supernatural and the woods of New England. Hawthorne was related to one of the judges during the Salem Witch Trial. Several buildings associated with Hawthorne, including the Custom House and the House of Seven Gables, have been linked to ghostly activity. And, Hawthorne himself reportedly spotted a ghost while spending time in the

Boston Athenaeum. Why wouldn't a hotel bearing his name be likewise haunted?

According to local lore, the hotel is indeed the source of some strange stories. In fact, many visitors and workers have reported that the site is just as haunted as any others in town.

One of the main hotspots in the hotel is the restaurant. Located on the first floor of the building, the restaurant is a delightful spot to dine or just pass time, complete with a nautical theme. A central piece of décor is the large ship's wheel that is hung in the restaurant. Some people have noticed that the wheel has an uncanny habit of moving on its own. Rocking back and forth, the wheel seems to be navigating the hotel to some unknown destination. When customers or staff attempt to stop the wheel from rocking, it pauses momentarily...then continues. While the phenomenon is not a common occurrence, the fact that it occurs suggests that, perhaps, some of the old captains who frequented the site might be coming back to sail once more.

Other parts of the hotel are also thought to be haunted. In a section called the Lower Deck, the staff has tried to set up tables and chairs for different functions. On a few occasions, when staff has left the room, the tables and chairs have been rearranged without explanation.

The Maritime Society, which still maintains headquarters at the top of the hotel, is also an occasional haunt for ghosts who pass through the night. According to members of the group, charts and maps that are kept in the locked room are often disorganized — maybe reorganized — without any known reason. Could it be the ghosts of the society's past are trying to check out their latest destination using nautical charts?

The hotel was featured on an episode of "Ghost Hunters." Members of the regional organization, TAPS, visited in an attempt to find evidence to explain the ghostly activity. Through the long process of searching rooms and checking the hotel, they were unable to record any evidence that would suggest a ghost inhabited the structure. That does not mean that something unexplainable might be happening at the hotel.

If you do have the chance to visit the Hawthorne Hotel, it is a treat. My wife Melissa and I had visited the restaurant before writing this book and she also was part of a function at the hotel. It's truly a grand place that conjures up images of the past. And, on our visits there, we must report that the only spirits that appeared in the restaurant were—in bottles and on tap. We have not had any supernatural experiences there...at least not yet.

5

Salem's Haunted Cemetery

The Howard Street Cemetery

The History

The Howard Street Cemetery in Salem, next to the old Salem Jail, is one of the oldest cemeteries in town. Although the exact date of its opening remains a mystery — some of the gravestones are undated — the earliest burial markers appear to date from 1809.

The Howard Street Cemetery is one of the lesser-known cemeteries in the city. There are no famous gravestones here... no Salem Witch trial victims, no distinct members of the China Trade. In fact, many of the people buried in the cemetery are actually children — most from the early 1800s, which is a sad testament to the youth mortality rate at the time. The marked gravestones range in dates from 1809 to 1878, though several have "unknown" listed where the date would go, suggesting the cemetery was used primarily in the nineteenth century.

The cemetery has its own unique charm. Most of the gravestones are in good shape, and trees are scattered throughout. The cemetery is wedged between an iron fence and the ancient (and former) Salem Jail. It forms a tight perimeter to the jail and presents itself as a foreboding presence amid modern complexes in the city.

The Howard Street Cemetery was the site where Giles Corey was pressed to death. His ghost is thought to inhabit the cemetery.

The Mystery

From the surface, the Howard Street Cemetery looks like any typical old New England burial ground. The scene is quiet and the grass is green, with various graves scattered throughout the yard. An old iron fence sets a fine perimeter for the mass of headstones. However, as with many cemeteries, things are rarely quite the way them seem.

The Howard Street Cemetery is one of the most haunted sites in the Witch City. People who visit are often initially overwhelmed as they approach the cemetery and often express an extreme sense of sorrow, distress, or power as they merely walk past the cemetery.

However, for some people, the experience does not just end with a strange feeling. Occasionally keen-eyed ghost hunters who happen to arrive at the cemetery on the right day might encounter something odd. For, it's believed that a variety of ghosts remain stuck in the cemetery—and do not intend to leave.

One of the more curious accounts of ghosts in the vicinity dates back to the days of the Salem Witch Trials. It's believed that Giles Corey, a victim of stone pressing, died on this ground.

Many of those who have reported paranormal experiences at the cemetery believe that he is the source of the haunting. His dour and sorrowful ghost — still angry at the unjust atrocity committed against him and the others of Salem — is believed to wander the cemetery from time to time. Legend has it that Corey makes a full manifestation when something is about to occur in Salem. Several witnesses claim that he appeared in the cemetery in 1814...shortly before a fire ravaged the city (more on this later).

Other spirits may also inhabit the cemetery. Occasionally, people speak about a woman spirit who has appeared there. Along with this, other passersby have been touched, poked, or felt a rush of cold air when passing near the cemetery.

> Author's Note: The gates to the cemetery are usually locked. There are entryways into the cemetery and signs indicating when the cemetery is open. Some sources have suggested that, at times, the cemetery has been closed to the public. Make sure to check the signs carefully for times when visitors can peruse the grounds.

The Haunted Jail of Salem

The History

One glance at the contemporary remnants of the jail and you automatically envision a classic Hollywood haunted building. Even if it wasn't haunted — or you didn't believe in ghosts — this building would make you think otherwise.

The Old Salem Jail was originally opened on Peter Street in 1813. For more than 150 years, the jail served as an official prison in Salem. The jail was built between 1811 and 1813. An addition was added to the building in the late 1800s to accommodate the number of prisoners.

Overlooking Howard Street Cemetery — a place considered one of the most haunted sites in Salem — the jail served generations of inmates. It once housed the Boston Strangler and played host to Harry Houdini, who was visiting the area. As time passed and other jails from the era closed, the Salem jail remained opened. Conditions at the jail worsened and, in 1991, the jail finally closed because it was unsuitable for occupation. Since that time, the jail has stood unoccupied...the jail is a decaying building, looking stark and cold. While the town hopes to sell the property for private use, it remains a silent remnant to an era goneby.

The old Salem jail has a legacy of hauntings. Just by glancing at the jail, you can see why. The gothic looking building is a quintessential haunt...even Hollywood would be proud.

The jail looks like a formidable building; a fortress, really, that holds a deep history. Lining the jail is an old chain link fence, wrapped in barbed wire and rusting with age. Beyond that, lies a

This gothic looking building is the Old Salem Jail. Some people still claim that Civil War ghosts can be spotted walking inside its halls.

second fence blanketed by the first, forming a tighter enclosure around the ancient building. Several of the bricks that permeate the structure are fading and a few have chips that look like they will one day erode into crumbles. Unkempt grass shoots up like wild weeds, making a scene that only the Munsters would love.

Yet, it's the deep inside of the building that holds the greatest mystery. For, according to legend, the old jail is home to lingering ghosts that seem imprisoned forever.

The Mystery

A host of stories have been told about this building. According to some people who have passed by the jail, strange sounds seem to echo off the walls...whispers or shouts of some unknown nature, leading many people to believe that former prisoners still inhabit the grounds.

Some people even believe that ghosts used to pass through the walls, *taunting prisoners* who were in jail. A few of these people claim that the ghosts belong to those of former Civil War prisoners. The jail served as home to many prisoners during the war, and the cramped conditions made for less than favorable conditions.

Other people have looked at the windows of the old building and noticed some unusual things: *strange shadows* and *an occasional figure* have been spotted. At other times, lights have been seen glowing from deep within the building—even though electricity no longer runs through the vacant place.

Ghosts have also been spotted *outside* the jail. On occasion, spirits of prisoners have been seen wandering through the overgrown lawn, peering near the barbed wire fences. Orbs of light have also been spotted in pictures taken around the jail.

There's no doubt that something peculiar is occurring at the jail. Whatever the source, there is little doubt that the jail might still imprison people to this day.

Author's Note: The jail has long been abandoned and is locked. The area is closed to any visitor.

7

A Customary Ghost

The Custom House Ghost

The History

In the early 1800s, the United States began commerce with Asian countries. China became one of America's biggest trade partners. With a vast array of goods and spices, items from China became a sought after commodity in America, and soon the China Trade was sweeping the nation.

In the mid 1800s, Salem became a major center for this China Trade. Ship captains who called Salem home made fortunes from importing and exporting goods to the Asian countries and, with large fortunes amassed, they built sizeable estates on the oceanfront to showcase their extreme wealth.

One of the most glorious streets to visit in Salem is Derby Street. Many of the houses are period mansions, complete with ornate decorations and elaborate design. These glorious manses magnify the spectacle of the China Trade.

Among the buildings on Derby Street lies the Custom House. Built in 1819, the building embodies the architecture of the Federalist period. Perley Putnam, a weigher and gauger for the United States Custom Department, developed the original design for the building a year earlier and supervised its construction, which cost a hefty $10,000 at the time. The building was placed near Derby Wharf, the major destination of ships returning to Salem. The Custom House was where taxes were levied on imports into the country. It's estimated that at one time upwards of twelve percent of the taxes paid in America passed through this building.

The old Salem Custom House is believed to be haunted. Nathaniel Hawthorne once worked in the Custom House and is believed to have spent his spare time there writing *The House of Seven Gables*.

Over time, the structure has gained fame for other reasons. It plays a prominent role in the introductory chapters of Nathaniel Hawthorne's *The Scarlet Letter* and there's good reason for that: Hawthorne worked as an inspector at the Custom House from 1846 to 1849. Some scholars theorize that he wrote a generous portion of his manuscript while passing down time in the building. Apparently, the novel writing had an effect on Nathaniel—Hawthorne was fired from the job for allegedly spending so much time writing when he was supposed to be working.

The Custom House was the thirteenth and last such building to be constructed in Salem. The large building was maintained by the U.S. Customs Department until 1936, and has since become part of the National Park Service. It stands today opposite Derby Wharf, still watching over the Salem shore that it once ruled.

The Mystery

The building may have a place in literary history, but it also plays a role in local lore as well...many visitors think that that the Custom House is haunted.

Exactly who plies the halls of the centuries old building remains unknown, but visitors and workers alike have reported some unusual experiences over the years. For most people, the supposed ghosts manifest themselves in the form of voices permeating the halls. The voices tend to be gruff, causing ghost enthusiasts to suggest they belong to sailors of old. There, the ghosts perhaps reminisce about the past fortunes they made or treasures that they found.

Other people report hearing strange footsteps echo through the hall. These footsteps seem to hint at sailors or other men walking through the building, perhaps waiting for their next turn in line. On occasion, glowing orbs have been spotted floating through the Custom House, hinting that unearthly visitors have arrived. And, odd lights are sometimes seen casting an eerie glow inside the building.

The building is open for tours from the National Park Service. You can wander through the building and revisit a part of history. But, don't be disappointed if you ask the rangers about the unearthly visitors. Park guides typically refrain from mentioning the ghostly tales or discussing if the building is actually haunted.

Author's Note: Salem's Custom House is located on Derby Street (opposite Derby Wharf). It's maintained and run by the National Park System as one part of the Salem Maritime National Historic Site.

Old Burial Point Cemetery

The Oldest Cemetery in Town

The History

*I*n the year 1637, the town of Salem decided to construct its first cemetery. The town hoped to choose a secluded spot that would serve as an ideal final resting place for the town's departed. Choosing the spot proved easy; town members agreed that a small spot on the banks of the South River was perfect. It was sheltered, it was quaint, and it had probably already served as a de facto cemetery for several of the town's deceased since 1628. So, it was no surprise that the town's first official cemetery of the time period opened there.

The cemetery proved useful for a variety of purposes. Not only was it a burial ground, it was also the site of a windmill, erected by John Home, as well as a cattle pasture that was granted to John Cromwell several years later.

The picturesque cemetery, on Charter Street, expanded a few times over its nearly 375-year history. And, it in that time it has also seen several famous occupants. Some of the residents that have been interned here include:

❖ **Anne Bradstreet** — A renowned poet of Massachusetts, her lyrical love poems are still popular to this day.

❖ **Simon Bradstreet** — Married to Anne Bradstreet, he served as a governor of Massachusetts. Family members eventually sold his tomb and his remains were moved to a new location.

❖ **Bartholomew Gedney** — He served as one of the judges on the Salem Witch Trials.

❖ **John Hathorne** — Another one of the judges at the Salem Witch Trials, he lived on the land that was later used to build Danvers State Hospital.

❖ **Samuel McIntire** — A wood carver and building designer in Salem, he was so skillful that many of the town merchants used his designs on their houses. McIntire also helped design the old Registry of Deeds and Salem Courthouse. An entire district in the town is dedicated to his architecture.

❖ **Richard More** — One of the first people to live in the thirteen colonies, he arrived on the Mayflower in 1620. More represents one of the handfuls of Pilgrim Fathers who eventually left Plymouth to settle the extremities of modern Massachusetts. He became a mariner and sea captain. His gravestone is believed to be the only Pilgrim stone to be laid at the actual date of burial (between 1694 and 1696, though his headstone lists 1692, suggesting someone has attempted to carve over it.)

❖ **Nathaniel Mather** — He is more famously known as the brother of Reverend Cotton Mather, the puritanical leader, whose fire and brimstone beliefs stoked the fire of strict laws of early Massachusetts.

❖ **John Turner** — A ship captain, he built the structure better known as the House of Seven Gables.

The burial ground may be home to some of Salem's finest...yet, it also has another significant claim to fame. Nathaniel Hawthorne, Salem native and writer extraordinaire, was fond of wandering through graveyards and frequented this cemetery. He even borrowed names from the headstones and incorporated them into his stories, most notably the name "Dr. Swinnerton;" a character with this name appears in the book *The House of Seven Gables*.

The Mystery

While the Old Burial Point Cemetery may hold a claim to fame as the oldest cemetery in town — and perhaps the second oldest cemetery in the country — it also may hold another claim to fame. It might be the home of an unusual ghost that haunts Salem.

The cemetery has been the site of the occasional ghostly appearance of a lady in white. The ghost itself does not typically appear in person. Rather, it often manifests itself in the form of orbs. It has even appeared as a slight figure on pictures taken at the site.

No one seems to know who this figure is. While it may be the figure of a woman associated with the Salem Witch Trials, it may also be one of the countless historical figures that may inhabit the cemetery.

9

Salem's Haunted Island

Legends of Baker's Island

The History

To borrow from a well-known advertising campaign: with a name like Baker's, it's got to be good. As many people who have spent time on Baker's Island know, the tiny isle is a little piece of paradise. The island is a quiet getaway for generations of homeowners who have called the island their vacation escape.

In fact, Baker's Island is a popular spot to vacation. The island is a sixty-acre parcel of land about three miles off shore from Salem, dotted with various kinds of cottages—many that have been passed down through generations for more than one hundred years. The island is a neat summer community that has developed a close bond during those years. Besides cottages, the island town contains a store, meeting hall, fire station, and gift shop.

The history of Baker's Island is intertwined with the maritime history of Salem. The island became a part of Salem in 1660 when the Massachusetts's government asked the seaport to care for the island. The purpose of the island was to provide wood and shelter to nearby fishermen. In the 1690s, the town of Salem appointed a caretaker to the island to prevent people from surrounding towns, particularly Marblehead, from arriving on the shores of the island and taking wood. Despite reasonable efforts to do this, Baker's Island was quickly deforested.

In the late 1670s, a merchant named John Turner purchased the island. He built a summerhouse on the island. Turner probably frequented the island until 1683, when Massachusetts used the island as a storehouse for cotton from Barbados. Because a smallpox epidemic had hit the Caribbean nation, Salem officials unloaded the cotton on Baker's Island to prevent the disease from spreading.

The island stayed in the Turner family until 1770. Several owners held title to the island while the government constructed two lighthouses on the isle. The lighthouses provided safe guidance for ships entering the harbor, particularly on stormy nights. The beacons remained an important part of the island for centuries, and one lighthouse remains intact to this day.

In the 1800s, the island became a tourist spot. Nathan Morse, a doctor who believed in alternative remedies, opened a hotel and spa on the island in 1888. The resort provided the ideal escape that many Bostonians needed. Here, people could fish, sail, play golf, or take part in many different activities coordinated by Morse.

The hotel remained opened until it was burned by a fire in 1906. By that time, Baker's Island had become a popular tourist destination. Small houses and cottages were built on the island. Many of these homes remain to this day.

The Mystery

And, while a name like Baker's Island does suggest a special type of sweetness, when paired with the fact that Baker's Island is part of the "Misery Island" chain in Salem, there isn't the slightest doubt this side of Stephen King that there has to be something unique about the island. And...*there is.*

Baker's Island is home to many different supposed haunts that have permeated the solute atmosphere during the past century and a half. While the ghosts have only shown themselves to certain people at certain times, there are many people who believe that at some point in time "something strange" may have happened on the shores of this docile island.

The best known sighting involves the ghost of a woman who wanders the island, as if looking for a lost loved one. According to rumors, the ghost belongs to a woman who had visited the island and passed through the marshland. Somehow, she got stuck in the wetlands and perished there. However, her ghost may linger and she may still be in search of a way off the island. There have been reports that she has appeared, dressed in flowing white attire, walking throughout the island. Some believers suggest she has even visited cottages hoping to find someone who could help her.

Another ghost that supposedly haunts the island belongs to that of a horse. That's right — a horse. Apparently, there was a horse that lived near the Baker Island lighthouse. This horse died in the middle of the night — perhaps a result of a sudden storm. Not one to leave the world quietly, this horse's spirit is said to have lingered on near the lighthouse. There, some visitors say, they have heard the ghostly bray of a horse at night, whinnying solemnly in the still nighttime air.

A third ghost believed to roam the island may have a slightly mischievous plan in mind. According to an article on the Internet-based newsletter *The Scarlet Letter, Whispers from the Witch City of Salem, Massachusetts,* writer Angela Brim mentions that the ghost of a jewel thief has been spotted on the island. The thief has appeared on some nights when there's a full moon, scouring the island for his well-hidden treasure...a treasure that seems to have gone missing — if it exists at all — for years.

Other ghostly sightings have been attributed to the island as well. The sounds of an ancient party—complete with laughter and clanging glasses—have been heard from time to time on the island. It is perhaps a party left over from years goneby.

While Baker's Island remains a quiet resort to this day, there is certainly no doubt that something peculiar may still linger on the island.

Author's Note: The Island, which is part of the Misery Island Group, is comprised of mainly private cottages and houses. Visitors are reminded to respect all rules of the island and respect residents' privacy.

10

Salem's Haunted Dungeon

The Witch Dungeon Musuem,
Lynde Street

The History

*I*magine it is 1692 and life in Salem Village is unfolding before your eyes. Girls are behaving strangely. Panic and fear grip a village witnessing an unknown phenomenon. The unbending will of Puritanical judges searching for evil rules the village. It all comes to life...in the Witch Dungeon Museum in Salem.

The Witch Museum has operated in the Witch City since 1979. Offering tourists and school children the opportunity to witness the Salem Witch Trials up close, the museum attempts to portray the harsh reality that was Massachusetts in 1692.

In what may be viewed as a true bit of natural historical irony, the museum itself was reconstructed out of what appears to be a nineteenth century church. Here, actors take the stage and present the trial of accused witch Sarah Good, one of several women to be accused and hanged for witchcraft in Salem. Spectators watch as trial participants' hearsay, illusion, and invisible evidence combine to incriminate yet another trial victim in this popular museum show.

Following the show, visitors can actually descend into the basement depths — or rather dungeon — of the museum that is dressed in darkness and designed to resemble the seventeenth century Salem Village. Complete with fifteen scenes featuring

Reverend Parris's household, the old Salem Jail, Gallow's Hill, and a local forest, Salem's witchcraft legacy comes alive with an indelible power that lingers in the hearts and minds of people who visit. The Witch Dungeon Museum is often heralded as one of the more popular attractions in town and one that leaves people thinking and talking about the many different witch trials that have occurred in America's history.

The Mystery

Now, if a museum set aside to depict the Salem Witch Trials isn't enough to stoke the imagination, then a unique legacy of the museum certainly might...for beneath its educational and theatrical appearance lies a slight mystery that has been passed down over time.

According to people who have worked at the institution in the past, as well as some who have visited, the Witch Dungeon Museum has its own extra attraction hiding amid the scenes in the cellar. It just might have a ghost.

For years, stories of mysterious occurrences inside the museum have permeated the North Shore. Ghost book author Holly Mascot Nadler noted that shortly after the museum opened, actors reported a chair *rocking* in one of the cellar scenes. The actors often left the scene of the mysterious rocking chair and, more than once, stated that they had seen a spirit, dressed in a cloak, wandering the basement as well.

At the time, only a few people knew that the dungeon had actually served as a church in the past. However, as that knowledge became more common, and the hooded figure was seen more often, the spirit was associated with a former monk who might have worked at the church in the past. Exactly who the monk might be, no one knows. What his reason for visiting the haunted sites below that wreak of a sad and harsh past seems even more baffling. While he's not commonly spotted in the museum, according to author Lynda Lee Macken, he is typically spotted near the scene depicting Giles Corey's death... itself an event that has given way to its own Salem legends.

So the next time you make a stop to the Salem Witch Dungeon Museum, remember that you might not just be witnessing the recreation of history. You just might catch a glimpse of some real history in the making.

11

Salem's Haunted Inn

The Stephen Daniels House

The History

*S*tephen Daniels was a ship captain during the early days of Salem's maritime trade. A Salem resident, he built a home in 1667 that still stands today. As with many of the older houses in New England, the Daniels house was passed through several generations of Daniels, who added onto the abode.

The house remained in the Daniels family until 1931. It remained unoccupied until 1945, when a family turned the house into a guest inn with a tearoom. They ran the house as an inn until the 1960s, when a woman named Kay Gill purchased the property.

Gill turned the property into the Stephen Daniels Inn, which operates as a bed and breakfast in the sea town. The inn is considered the oldest in Salem. And, it retains much of its old-style charm. The rooms are decorated with antiques that reflect the classic colonial period in North Shore's history. The inn is a spot that makes memories special for visitors to the city.

The Mystery

The Stephen Daniels house still retains some of its old time charm. However, it may hold a little bit more as well. As author Mark Jasper found out while doing research for his book *Haunted Inns of New England*, the Stephen Daniels house may also be the home of some old time ghosts.

According to Jasper, at least three different ghosts are thought to reside at the inn:

❖ A man who has manifested at least once and bears a striking resemblance to the portrait of a man that hangs on one of the inn's walls;

❖ A woman who visits the inn. At least one guest to the inn has seen the woman descend one of the staircases inside the house. It should be noted that the ghost appears none too nimble; or perhaps there have been renovations since the first time she set foot in the Daniels house...for the ghost has been known to fall down the stairs as she attempts to descend them.

❖ Perhaps the most intriguing ghost believed to inhabit the inn is that at of a gray and black striped cat. The feline has been seen roaming the inn, wandering in and out of rooms, often stopping to rest on beds. Jasper notes that the cat once snuggled up next to an unsuspecting guest, who felt something strange resting beside her one night but no one and no thing was there. She later deduced that it was the ghost cat that had come to visit during the night. And, on some occasions, people have left plates of milk out for the cat, hoping to provide the gentle creature a tasty treat.

Who or what the haunts are remains anyone's guess. The human ghosts may be former Daniels' family members or their friends—and the cat perhaps belonged to the Daniels at one point in time. What might be most interesting about the cat is that it bears an uncanny resemblance to the picture of a cat that Kay Gill painted and has hung in the inn. Ironically, Gill has never seen any of the ghosts herself, and certainly had no idea what the ghost cat purportedly looks like. The fact that she painted a cat so eerily similar to the one that haunts the inn is one of those unusual twists of fate...and which is not atypical of the landmarks in Salem.

12

Salem's Haunted Mansion

The Ropes Mansion, Essex Street

The History

uilt by the Ropes family in 1727, the beautiful Ropes Mansion has played a role in the history of Salem for nearly three centuries. The Ropes family was one of the first families to inhabit the coastal town, arriving in Salem in 1630.

The house, also called the Orne-Ropes Mansion, was built as the main home for a family that gained fame in Salem. The mansion was the birthplace of several accomplished merchants, writers, and sailors. The house itself became a showplace for the day and one room was even used to display items that were purchased from merchant ships visiting Asia.

While most of the days in the house were prosperous, less pleasant times managed to infiltrate the home in the early 1770s. At a time when tensions were high between New England and the mother country of England, colonists began choosing sides. Those who hoped for independence from England became outspoken Patriots and those who preferred continuing their present life became staunch Loyalists. While Salem was a hotbed for Patriot fervor, most of the Ropes family remained loyal to the crown.

Needless to say, this caused quite a stir in town. Legend has it that a group of radical Patriots decided to barge into the Ropes mansion in 1774 and hang the head of the family, none other than the well-known (at the time) judge Nathaniel Ropes, who was a magistrate in the probate and superior courts. Supposedly finding the elder Ropes in a fragile state, the townsfolk opted

to dispose of the hangman's noose and let the man live out his final days.

While no one knows if this story is true, it is believed that Nathaniel's sons were divided over the revolutionary activity of the time. When it became clear that neither son would budge from his beliefs, one of the sons — a Patriot — decided to leave the state. From then on, the mansion passed to various family members — including at least two other Nathaniels — until the late 1893, when the remaining tenants were three elderly women who had no children. The last of the women, Mary Pickman Ropes and Eliza Orne Ropes, willed the mansion to the Essex Museum. The museum owned the mansion until the 1970s, when the Peabody Essex Museum decided to purchase the edifice and add it to the historic collection of buildings they owned.

The mansion has evolved over time. The original architecture reflects a Dutch style that was popular in the colonies. A new doorway was added to the stately manse around 1805. The entire mansion was first renovated in 1894, when it was moved away from the street, and then a garden was added to the exterior in 1912. This garden serves as a prominent feature and a "can't miss" attraction for those who visit.

The Mystery

One of the early homeowners of the Ropes mansion was named Nathaniel Ropes. He and his wife Abigail inhabited the building in the late 1700s.

While Nathaniel is believed to have cheated death with those fervent Patriots who wanted his head, it's also believed that tragedy struck the Ropes family during their tenure in the home. One night, Abigail was in an upstairs room. As she was walking by her fireplace, her nightgown caught the edge of the logs. A quick spark shot onto her gown and within seconds it was ablaze. Abigail met an unfortunate death when the fire could not be put out in time.

While Abigail is thought to have died in her room, some people believe she still roams the halls on occasion. Several visitors to the mansion claim to have seen a woman wandering the top halls of the building. She appears to be dressed in nightclothes, searching for someone or something.

The home is now maintained and operated by the Peabody Essex Museum in Salem. People who visit still claim to feel a presence as they wander the halls…a reminder that the Ropes family may still linger in their home long after most people thought they had left.

13

Salem's Haunted Lot

The Curse of Giles Corey

Now, I know what you are thinking. How on earth can someone see a curse? Well, there are places where it has been seen to unfold... mainly in the old Salem's sheriff office. Read on:

The History

Sheriff George Corwin was a harsh man. Of this there is no doubt. Perhaps no one figure in the witchcraft trials might be forgotten and be misunderstood as this central figure in the Salem Witch Trials.

George Corwin was an unkind and rather feisty sheriff in Salem at the time of the witchcraft trials. Commonly hated — even reviled — by many in Salem, Corwin took his duties as a sheriff with seeming delight. About twenty-six years old at the start of the Salem witchcraft trials, he eagerly complied with the judges at the time, arresting several of Salem's villagers as supposed witches. It probably helped George Corwin that his father was Judge Jonathan Corwin, who presided over the trials in Salem. The elder Corwin helped his son obtain and keep the post that brought the Corwin name infamy.

Many historical texts suggest that Corwin proved particularly bothersome for those accused of witchcraft: he removed people from their beds in order to be detained, acted upon accusations that seemed to bear little evidence, and is believed to have beaten and tortured accused witches and their family members in order

to obtain confessions and information regarding their alleged activities.

Corwin's chief goal through the trials was to get a confession of some sort from the trial participants. Whether a plea of guilty or innocent, it did not matter to him. Corwin knew that either plea could allow all accused witches to lose their rights to their property if, indeed, they were found guilty when placed on trial. This happened several different times, and Corwin, as sheriff, took it upon himself to confiscate property when an accused witch was hanged, dividing the goods between himself and his deputies.

Corwin's reputation for claiming goods preceded him and when it came time for Giles Corey to be arrested, Corey knew full well what could happen to his earthly possessions. Corwin might claim the goods for himself if Corey entered a plea. So, Corey knew exactly what he had to do — say nothing.

This is exactly what Corey did. Each time Corwin tried to get Corey to issue a plea, Corey refused. Corwin probably tried some of his usual gifts for persuasion to get a confession of some sort from Corey...but Corey would not relent.

So, Corwin resorted to another trick of his trade, and one that is particularly nasty. He took Corey from the jail, stripped him of his clothes, and lay him down on a field. Then, he placed a large board — some sources consider it a door — over his chest and preceded to have stones placed on the board. Corwin assumed that such "pressing," as it was called, would prove unbearable and force Corey to speak.

However, Corey was unrelenting. As the stones mounted up, Corey refused to speak. Dumbfounded, and angered, Corwin ordered more stones to be put on the man. At one point, Corey's tongue began to hang out of his mouth as the weight proved too much. Unsympathetically, Corwin placed the tongue back in Corey's mouth with his stick, to ensure that the discomfort lasted as long as possible.

Eventually, Corwin could tell that Corey was near his end. He asked one last time for a confession. According to sources, Corey uttered a profanity at Corwin instead. Then, he reportedly snapped back, "I curse you, and Salem, too (or something to that effect)." Corwin was shocked and tried to get the confession one more time. Corey supposedly replied, "More weight." More weight was added, and Corey quickly succumbed, becoming the first, and only, accused witch to die by being pressed.

The Mystery

Corey's refusal to speak helped save his inheritance — which included various land holdings — for his family. Because Corwin could not get a plea, Corey's children had rights to claim his property and did so.

However, this is not the last that the world had heard from Giles Corey…or so many people say…for it's believed that Corey's curse might linger upon to this day.

Within four years of the end of the witchcraft trials, Corwin died. He seemed to have a bleeding fit that led to his demise — perhaps causing him to choke to death on blood — making historians theorize that he had a blood or heart ailment. Undoubtedly, it was an unusual end to a man who was considered fit and only thirty years old.

Yet, Corey's curse might not have been relegated to Corwin. According to author Robert Ellis Cahill, Corey's curse might have been attached to anyone who served as the sheriff of Salem or Essex County and was stationed at the old Salem Jail. As Cahill suggests, every known sheriff of the town stationed at the old jail had either suffered from, or died from, a heart or blood ailment—and Cahill should know this better than anyone because he served as sheriff of Salem and, you guessed it, retired because of a heart condition, a rare blood disease, and the fact that he had recently suffered a stroke. He did live on to write many a wonderful book about the local traditions and lore of New England.

Corey's curse might also have been transferred to the city of Salem as well. Many locals believe that the ghost of Giles Corey appears in the city during a time prior to great danger. Even Salem author Nathaniel Hawthorne made note of the unusual appearance of the ghost, stating that the apparition "of the wizard appears as a precursor to some great calamity impending over the community."

The reason for such a superstitious belief is that Corey's ghost has been spotted in the vicinity of the old Howard Street Cemetery—where he was pressed to death in years prior to its use as a burial ground—just before a variety of unusual incidents occurred that brought harm to the city for nearly 250 years. Often, he emerges in the cemetery appearing like the skeleton of a ghost, in tattered old clothes with a ghoulish expression. The last reported sighting was in 1914, when a slew of Corey sightings were noted right before a great fire that swept through the city.

Corey's curse may or may not be a real part of the city. Yet, needless to say, some people's words might just live on long after they have left this world.

14

Salem's Ghost Ship

The Saga of the Andrew Johnson

The History

*F*ishing is a dangerous business. A fisherman who decides to dedicate a life to the sea knows he or she will be at the mercy of the sea for days, even weeks at a time, hoping to make a haul that is worthy of the dangers. Wind, waves, and angry oceans all pose daunting threats for most fishermen. Because of this, fishing is not just an occupation...it's a religion.

There is no greater place to witness this religion in action than in the North Shore seaports of Massachusetts. From Glocuester, to Marblehead, to Salem and beyond, fleets of fishing boats have historically departed the pristine shores to gather fish in the Massachusetts Bay, the Grand Banks, and Georges Bank.

While a great many fishing boats have stories to tell, there are few in Massachusetts that have a story to tell quite like the *Charles Haskell*. The once locally famous schooner was built in the late 1860s for the purpose of cod fishing. The handsome schooner was supposed to be a marvel of the North Shore, but fate would play a role in changing that. Sometime between 1868 and 1869, right before taking her maiden voyage, the ship was ready for its final inspection when a worker (some stories say it was an inspector) slipped on the companion and eventually died from injuries suffered in a fall.

After mourning the loss of the worker and paying appropriate respects, other people might have shrugged off the tragedy and been ready to get the ship underway. But sailors, by nature, are a superstitious lot and, when it came time to hire a crew for the ship, there were few takers. No one wanted to work on a ship that had already seen one death without even voyaging away from the docks. Even locating a captain proved particularly difficult.

Within a year, a man named Captain Curtis of Gloucester agreed to man the ship. Curtis managed to gather a crew and the ship was ready for its maiden voyage in the later winter of 1869. It set off then with scores of other ships, straight for the Georges Banks. There, the *Charles Haskell*, like other ships, engaged in gathering a tremendous haul of fish. But, as is the case with Mother Nature during late winter, storm clouds began to gather, winds began to whip, and waves began to build. There was no doubt that a late winter gale was mounting.

Other fishing ships began to turn about and head back to shore. The *Charles Haskell* soon joined the retreating fleet and before long the schooners were dodging each other in a frantic attempt to escape the storm.

Just as the *Charles Haskell* was making good headway, another ship, the *Andrew Johnson* from Salem, crossed its path. According to stories, Captain Curtis tried to evade the ship, but the inevitable happened. The *Charles Haskell* collided with the *Andrew Johnson*, ramming its side. To make matters worse, as the Salem ship took on water, it's believed that a wave pushed the *Charles Haskell* on top of the *Andrew Johnson*, causing it to quickly sink to the bottom, washing its twenty-six-man crew out to sea. The members of the *Charles Haskell* attempted to rescue the men from the Salem ship, but the waves and weather proved too daunting. Soon, the *Andrew Johnson* and its crew were casualties of the sea.

When the *Charles Haskell* managed to return to port, the crew reported the incident. At that time, the sunken ship was officially identified as the *Andrew Johnson* (no one knew which ship it was that sank until that time).

The Mystery

Many New England sailing voyages have resulted in such tragedy. However, the events that followed have etched the *Andrew Johnson* tragedy into a different realm.

Several months later, the *Charles Haskell* was out to sea again. The ship quickly returned to the Georges Bank area, scooping up fish. After about eight and a half weeks at sea, something strange happened one crisp, calm night. A soft darkness surrounded the ship as the moon shone across the water. Everything seemed

normal and peaceful until the two men on watch noticed a series of strange objects emerge from the water and move toward the ship.

Surprised, the men kept a close eye on the objects until they neared the ship. At once, the men realized the objects were actually heads — of men. Moments later, the heads reached the ship and before the watchmen knew it, the heads came out of the water. Soon, a group of spectral men climbed up the side of the ship and ebbed their way on deck.

The watchman alerted the captain of the intruders. Soon, the entire crew was awakened and on deck in time to see the unimaginable. Ghosts had taken a spot on their ship. A quick count soon unveiled that there were twenty-six ghostly men on the ship. And, they seemed to be trying to rig and bait invisible nets to be used in the ocean. When their task was apparently complete, the men filed off the side of the ship...one at a time.

Shocked by the events of the night, the captain and crew decided to head home. There was no sense risking any more bizarre events such as this. However, port was two days away, so the men would have to spend at least one more night on board the ship.

As fate would have it, the following night...the ghosts revisited the ship. They climbed aboard, attempted to bait nets, and then, once done, prepared to leave. They headed toward the bow of the ship and paused. As the first embers of sunlight ebbed across the morning sky, the ghosts apparently realized they were near their home. They cast a heavy gaze to the west, where Salem lay, then took a look at the helm, where the captain kept his course steady toward the city of Gloucester. Perhaps recognizing their home harbor, one of the ghosts looked at the others, motioned with its hand, and slowly descended from the bow of the ship. The others followed, heading into the morning sunlight in the direction of their former home. Soon, there was no doubt — the ghostly crew of the *Andrew Johnson* had visited the *Charles Haskell*.

When the *Charles Haskell* returned to the port of Gloucester, news of the supernatural event spread. Soon everyone had heard about the visitors that had joined the crew of the *Charles Haskell*. People throughout the North Shore were amazed at the story. Yet, many a sailor, knowing the superstitious ways of the sea, were none surprised that the crew of the *Andrew Johnson* had returned from the sea.

Because of the experience, sailors wanted nothing to do with the *Charles Haskell*. Despite the fact that there were plenty of sailors and not enough boats to be outfitted, the fishermen of Gloucester steered far from the haunted ship. According to author Josef Berger, one man named Joe Enos did volunteer to return with Captain Curtis to sea, reasoning that if they encountered the ghost crew again, they could offer them a ride home to Salem. However, Curtis thought better of the idea, and the captain and owners were unable to outfit the ship for several years. In time, the ship was believed to have been sold to an owner located in Digby, Nova Scotia. To this day, no one knows if those who sailed aboard the *Charles Haskell* when it was moored in Canada ever saw the crew of the *Andrew Johnson*.

The experience of the men aboard the *Charles Haskell* proved memorable. Even until their last days, crewmembers of the ship retold the story and swore that they had encountered the unearthly spectrals of the crew that had perished at sea. The December 2, 1920 obituary section of the *New York Times* mentions the death of John Winters, the last survivor of the *Charles Haskell*. The obituary also points out the story of the *Charles Haskell* and the "Flying Dutchman" tale that surrounded it. The death notice indicated that Winters told the tale of a ship that pursued the *Charles Haskell* until the day he died. To this day, Winters' story and those of the *Charles Haskell* and the *Andrew Johnson* live on as part of the rich lore that surrounds the New England seashore.

Salem Harbor was once teeming with large ships. Did the crew of the ghost ship *Andrew Johnson* try to return here?

15

Lights over Salem

The famous UFO picture of 1952

The History

The year was 1952. "High Noon" and "Singing in the Rain" proved to be smash hits at the box office. Dwight D. Eisenhower served as President of the United States. The New York Yankees won the World Series. *The Caine Mutiny* earned the Pulitzer Prize.

The Mystery

However, the year was also known for other things. In UFO circles, it was considered a year of a flap — a high number of UFO sightings. According to some sources, the year 1952 might have been the peak of the UFO sensation in the United States. More people reported seeing UFOs that year than at any time prior to it. Salem, Massachusetts was the site of one of the most famous reports to surface in the United States.

The day was July 16. Shal Alpert, a seaman for the U.S. Coast Guard was working in the photographic laboratory at the Salem Coast Guard Weather Office. At approximately 9:35 a.m., he noticed a strange light formation—four lights, in apparent elliptical formation, were hovering over the town. Alpert, unsure of the source of the light, found a colleague and showed him the lights as well. The lights had dimmed slightly by that time, but before they disappeared, Alpert was able to take a picture of them.

The picture itself has gone onto legendary status. It's one of the clearer UFO pictures captured from the decade and helps to symbolize the UFO sightings of the 1950s. In fact, no collection of UFO stories is complete without mention of the event and the photograph.

The photograph was sent to the United States Air Force for further study. Initially, the military believed that the lights in the photograph were actually the result of a double exposure. Upon further investigation, they concluded that the strange glow in the photograph might have been caused by the reflection of light on a window. This theory, which has been presented as the official explanation of the Salem UFO for some time, suggests that the camera Alpert used caught the reflection of overhead lights that were in the lab. The picture captured the exact image that Alpert had seen…but all of it was due to natural reasons. In fact, the government explained that many photographs of alleged UFOs had been filmed in such a way without anyone realizing. Apparently, the Salem UFO, like many others, was simply explained by (Thomas) Edison and a little electricity.

UFOs were once spotted over this power station in Salem. Was it really a flying saucer? Or were indoor lights the real cause?

There are many people who remain unsatisfied with that explanation to this day. It has even been suggested by some UFO enthusiasts that, later, other government officials studied the photograph a third time. After studying the photograph this time, some officials determined that that source of the lights that had been photographed could not be explained by conventional means. Whether or not this report is true is hard to determine…but true UFO believers think that there are unearthly means behind Salem's legendary picture.

Part Two: Danvers

Danvers presents itself as a quiet town in the midst of the larger North Shore cities. Unassuming, with a quiet charm, Danvers has a unique place in American history.

Danvers was settled in 1636 as part of the Salem settlement. Dubbed Salem Village, it grew as a small farming village. It would probably have been forgotten in history, except for a small event that occurred in 1692 that changed the life of the town forever. Although most people associate the city of Salem with the Salem Witch Trials, the tragic events initially unfolded in the village, and by the end of the witch-hunt, several citizens had been hanged as witches.

    Following the trials, the town disassociated itself with Salem Town (the larger Salem settlement). It changed its name to Danvers — its origin still obscure in history — and made its own history. Until recently, the town shunned its witch trial past, and instead was dominated by a shoe industry, a legendary state hospital, and an agricultural base that gave rise to the locally famous Danvers carrot and Danvers onion. In fact, Danvers prides itself on the onion tradition, and nicknames itself "Onion Town."

    Danvers history has spanned three centuries. That time has given rise to interesting, and unique, stories...stories that still linger to this day.

The Witchcraft Memorial site is located in Danvers. This town was originally called Salem Village and was the site of the original witchcraft fever.

16

The Ghosts of the Asylum

Danvers State Hospital,
Hawthorne Hill

The History

*I*n the late 1800s, a mental health crisis gripped Massachusetts. One of the state hospitals (then called "insane asylums") in South Boston had recently closed. The three other hospitals scattered throughout Massachusetts swelled as they began taking patients who had been forced out by the closure. Because of overcrowding conditions, which were believed to hamper efforts to help people suffering from mental illnesses, something had to be done.

The state of Massachusetts turned to a little known section of the North Shore to construct what was then called a "lunatic hospital." Located in a tucked away spot, far from the mainstream population, state officials hoped that the new hospital would be the ideal location for those suffering from mental illness. From those humbled beginnings, the State Lunatic Hospital at Danvers was open.

Work on the building began in 1874. Under the guidance of renown architect Nathaniel J. Bradlee (the designer of the Lynn Water Works, the Hotel St. Cloud, and Trinity Church, well known places of the day), a large spread was built on a seventy-two acre section of Danvers known as Hawthorne Hill (at the time, it may have been known as Hathorne Hill). It gained this name because it once belonged to Judge Hathorne of Salem Witch Trial fame

and who was a distant relative of Nathaniel Hawthorne. Bradlee's design was a sprawling edifice meant to house many residents. The structure, known for its castle-like appearance that dominated the surrounding area, stood for years as a guardian over Route 1, looking down upon the surrounding landscape like an imposing vulture. The main structure was called the Kirkbride Building and was known for its large tower structure that shot up from the rest of the edifice.

The hospital opened in 1878, designed for institutional care of those suffering from mental illness. It based its design on Dr. Thomas Story Kirkbride, who believed that a variety of therapies and tranquil settings was the best way to help patients. His philosophy prescribed a rural setting, opportunities for work, and low patient numbers as a way to enhance the quality of life. The Danvers State Hospital successfully used the ideas to help many patients.

Over time, the purpose of the hospital evolved. In 1899, a nursing school was added to the site, providing training opportunities for those who might want to work with patients suffering from mental illness. About twenty-one years later, the hospital began setting up a diagnostic center for children. The purpose was to identify children who might be suffering from mental illness. Other buildings were added on the site to house an influx of patients and increased activities at the site.

The hospital continued its work until the 1960s. By that time, the hospital began to suffer. The facility was slowly growing outdated. The number of patients swelled to 2,500 people, which led to a vast overcrowding situation. At the same time, medicine and attitudes toward mental illness began to shift. The use of newer outpatient therapies caused the population at the state hospital to dwindle. Slowly, but surely, the old system became as outdated as the building. By the 1980s, several stories painted an unpleasant picture of life at Danvers State Hospital. Lawsuits that cited inadequate care for some of the patrons and stories of patients being released when perhaps they should not have been began to circulate, whether grounded in fact or not. In 1992, the State Hospital eventually was closed, due to a lack of funding.

Following the closure of the hospital, attempts were made to identify uses for the building. In 2001, the building was the spooky backdrop for a horror movie called "Session 9" starring David Caruso. The movie tells the tale of a man who goes insane while removing asbestos from the hospital. According to an article on the website,

AboutFilm.com, Caruso himself felt chills while filming in the old hospital, calling it "the scariest building in North America."

In 2003, AvalonBay Community developers began an effort to purchase the site and demolish buildings on the hill to construct private housing. At the time, the proposal raised many eyebrows. Some people hoped to preserve the historic structure that had long been part of the tapestry of the North Shore. Others wondered if people would actually choose to live on the grounds of a former state hospital. In the end, AvalonBay was able to purchase the property and built private housing on it. The group agreed to incorporate some of the original Kirkbride structure in the final design. However, the sale remained in the air because of lawsuits and disagreements between community members, historic organizations, and the state.

In 2004, in the midst of the property dispute, a mysterious fire gutted part of the original structure that had been badly dilapidated by time and weather. Shortly after, AvalonBay persevered in their endeavor to purchase the property. Despite protests throughout the region, AvalonBay razed some of the thirty-nine structures on the site, while preserving the Kirkbride Building, which was on the National Register of Historic Places. They also preserved two of the cemeteries that existed on the site, which were the final resting place of hospital residents. While construction progressed, an odd fire wrecked three of the newly constructed buildings in 2007 — before people had moved in. The source of the blaze has never been determined. However, when all was said and done, the AvalonBay condominium and apartment complex was eventually built on the land.

The Mystery

There is no doubt that Danvers State Hospital has a unique place in the history of the North Shore and indeed all of Massachusetts. However, as a paranormal hotspot, it might be beyond compare. Several people and websites have labeled the former state hospital as "the most haunted place in Massachusetts."

The exact nature of the haunts came in many shapes and forms. Some came from former employees, workers, and ghost enthusiasts who illegally trespassed on the property, after it had been closed, in search of alleged ghosts. The area was heavily patrolled and most of these ghost hunters who trespassed were stopped before they could do harm to themselves in the buildings that were slowly disintegrating.

Most of the actual ghost sightings are attributed to the departing energy of those who lived at the hospital, particularly during the days when overcrowded conditions led to a less than pleasant environment at the hospital.

While several of the stories are nebulous, some are quite convincing. Newswriter Michael Puffer narrated several tales in a *Danvers Herald* article in 2003 based on his interviews with people interested in the hospital. According to his article, one woman who lived on the site because her father worked at the hospital had several encounters with the spirits when she was younger. She had witnessed the ghost of an older woman at the top of her stairs one day and remembers having sheets tugged off the bed on occasion. Although she never felt that the ghosts were malicious, she definitely felt that they were present.

The article also mentions that other people who had visited the site before it was closed heard unusual noises. They often felt a strong energy on the hilltop location. Most ghost researchers believe that the energy is leftover from the period of sadness, hopelessness, and grief associated with the overcrowding. These energies have been magnified over time and felt to this day.

However, many of the strongest ghost stories may never be known. When the hospital was closed, trespassing was frequent on the site of the gothic hospital. Frequent police patrols helped eradicate the problem. Because of the unwanted interest in the building, ghost hunting became frowned upon; as a result, many people who study spirits were never able to check out this building.

Now that the site is private housing, people no longer visit the site to check out the energy and see the spooky buildings. In fact, now that Hawthorne Hill has been used for a different purpose, there have been no public reports of anything out of the ordinary occurring in the houses located there. Perhaps the spirits that had haunted the land were happy to see that it was now being put to a better use. They may have made peace with their old life and moved on to a new one—as some ghosts are thought to do—far from the old Danvers State Hospital.

17

Danvers' Spirited Bookworm

An Urban Legend:

The Ghost
of the Peabody Institute Library

This tale is considered an urban legend, as no one is too sure where it occurred or who has spotted the ghost mentioned here. I've been to the library many times and know many others who also have been...yet no one has spotted this ghost. But it's a tale so well known in the Internet community that it's worth including. Read on:

The History

*M*ost libraries are a book lover's dream, but the Peabody Institute Library in Danvers is a step above — it is an architect's dream as well. The building, designed to look like a Georgian revival mansion, initially seems more suited as a Hollywood home than a warehouse of knowledge.

The Peabody Institute Library has a long history in the town of Danvers. Now, you might wonder how a town named Danvers might have a library named for a town next door (that is, if you know that Peabody is the name of the neighboring town). And, while that might seem like a logical question, the local library of Oniontown is hardly named for the neighbor—it's named for a man named George Peabody.

George Peabody, a wealthy banker and local philanthropist, believed that the town should have a library. Peabody donated $10,000 for the establishment of a library in South Danvers in 1856. A hefty sum at the time, the money was used to purchase books and set up a library in the Danvers Town Hall.

Though popular, the library eventually was on the move. In 1857, the town purchased land on Sylvan Street that they hoped would house a building specifically designed to be a library. In 1866, Peabody donated another hefty sum — this time $40,000 — for the establishment of a building to serve as the library. After three years of construction, the library opened in what is known as Peabody Park. The Gothic structured garnered a lot of praise throughout the community.

The initial building served the town well for twenty-one years. In July 1890, a fire destroyed the building. The trustees of the library sought to honor Peabody's legacy and rebuild the building. Using an estimated $23,600 in insurance money, construction on the current Georgian revival building began. In 1892, the building was complete at a cost of a little more than $34,000 and opened to the public. It was a magnificent structure of the day, complete with an auditorium on the second level that could hold more than 1,000 people.

Over the past century, the library has been gradually expanded and renovated. The auditorium has been reclaimed to make more room for books. A children's room and archival center were added to the basement of the building.

Currently, the building stands as a gem in the town, and a legacy of learning and literature in the small North Shore town.

The Mystery

What would any library be without a little story to it? Well, like many libraries, the Peabody Institute seems to have its own tale—and it's not one told in the books at the library. According to Internet lore,

The Peabody Institute Library in Danvers is home to a variety of books and archival center. Is it home to a ghost as well?

there are people who believe that the spirit of a past patron inhabits the library. Some people have reported that the ghost of an elderly gentleman has emerged in the reading rooms on the third floor of the library. He appears to be a kind gentleman who appreciates the respectful atmosphere of the library—and he's been known to shush anyone who makes too much noise.

Whether or not there is an actual ghost in the building — or who it might be if there is one — remains unknown. Perhaps the report started with someone who watched the opening salvo of "Ghostbusters" one too many times. On our visits to the library, no ghost emerged from the woodwork or the stacks, and there haven't been many reports to suggest a ghost exists there, either. However, only time will tell if the Peabody Institute will have a ghost that checks in the books permanently.

Now, before people start wondering if books aren't the only thing to check out at the Peabody Library, one source can probably best set the record straight. According to an email from Richard Trask, a life-long resident of Danvers and town archivist who knows anything about anything Danvers, the story of the ghost might be as much pure fiction as the titles on the shelves. Trask says that he worked in the library at the Archival Center and never once heard of a ghost haunting the upper levels.

It appears that the thoughts of a ghost may be a case — or perhaps book cover — closed.

18

The Ghost of Rebecca Nurse

The Rebecca Nurse Homestead

The History

The Rebecca Nurse homestead is a seventeenth century house that has stood for more than three hundred years. Located on twenty-five acres in current day Danvers, the Rebecca Nurse homestead was once part of a three hundred-acre parcel of land given to Townsend Bishop in 1636. The property stayed in Bishop's hands until it was sold to the governor of the colony, Endecott Peabody, in 1648. Peabody improved the property — which was by then located in Salem Village — and lived there for a short period of time. The property passed through at least one other owner by the 1670s, James Allen, who leased the property to the Nurse (sometimes called Nourse) family in 1678.

Francis Nurse is believed to have built part of the house that currently stands on the homestead property shortly after he signed a twenty-year lease to use the property. Nurse settled on the land with his wife Rebecca and their eight children, farming the land and raising livestock.

Life was fairly normal at the Nurse family homestead for thirteen years, but, in the winter of 1691 and 1692, times changed in the village. With the advent of the Salem Witch Trials, almost anyone in the village was in danger of being accused of witchcraft—and Rebecca Nurse was no exception. On March 19, 1692, the girls who had been accusing people of witchcraft pointed their collective finger at Rebecca Nurse, declaring that she was a witch.

The accusation of Nurse caused major friction in the town. At the age of 71, Rebecca Nurse was well known and respected by many townsfolk. However, as factions began to divide in town, the Nurse family squarely came on the side of those who disagreed with the witch trials. Perhaps because of this, the allegations against Nurse stuck. She was arrested — many believe in her bed — on March 23.

Nurse was tried for her alleged crime of witchcraft that June. The testimony against her was particularly sketchy. The girls' accusations were the major testimony that was used against her. These accusations were corroborated by the testimony of a neighbor whose property bordered the Nurse homestead. For years, the two families quarreled about roaming livestock. When Rebecca got particularly upset that one of the cows became loose on her property, the Holten family found it odd that the cow started acting strangely after that. So, they believed it was the work of Nurse.

The testimony did not satisfy the judges of the trial. And, when forty of Rebecca's neighbors and friends signed a petition, testifying to her character, there was no doubt about it. Rebecca was found not guilty.

But...the times were strange in the village. The girls reacted bizarrely to the claim of innocence, breaking out into crying fits of terror. Their fits of unusual behavior returned, and the chief justice soon asked his judges to reconsider. They did. Nurse, who was originally found not guilty, became a victim of double jeopardy. The judges sentenced her to hang. Despite repeated attempts by her children to save her, Nurse was hanged July 19, 1692.

Following her hanging, Nurse's body was buried near the gallows of Salem. Because she was accused of being a witch, she was not allowed a proper burial. Needless to say, her children felt a strong disdain toward the legal system in Salem. So, under the cloak of darkness, they went to Gallow's Hill and retrieved their mother's body. They buried her in an unmarked grave near the Nurse homestead.

Francis died in 1695, and the homestead passed through several tenants. It stayed in the Nurse family through the 1770s, and was owned by a great-grandson named Francis, who fought in the Revolutionary War and saw action at the Battle of Lexington and Concord. After the war, the house was bought by Phineas Putnam and stayed in the Putnam family until 1908. The Rebecca Nurse Memorial Association purchased the house at that time, helping to

The Rebecca Nurse House of Danvers was once the home of an accused witch. Some people think it might now be the home of a ghost.

restore it, and currently the Danvers Alarm List Company, the local Revolutionary War re-enactors organization, owns and maintains the property.

The homestead has a long and proud heritage. It includes three separate buildings: the Nurse homestead, which includes seventeenth and eighteenth century architecture; a barn built around the frame of a house that was constructed in 1681; and a replica of the meetinghouse used during the Salem Witch Trials. The Nurse family cemetery, located down the hill from the main structures, helps complete the property. It houses gravestones for many Nurse family members, a gravestone for what is believed to be the remains of accused witch George Jacobs Sr. (whose remains were brought to the site in 1992), and a memorial to Rebecca Nurse whose gravesite has long remained hidden. The property has been a valuable resource for movies and documentaries about the Salem Witch Trials, including "Young Goodman Brown" and "Seven Sovereigns for Sarah." The homestead is open to tour groups, as well as Alarm List Company activities and encampments. It's also home to the annual Strawberry Festival in Danvers.

The Mystery

A house with such history would be an obvious site for supernatural activity. Ironically, there have been few stories connecting the homestead to any ghostly activity, which suggests that the turmoil-filled past that surrounds the homestead may still remain in the past. In fact, so many people have visited, volunteered, or camped on the area that it would seem certain that something unusual would have been seen. But no reports of ghosts have ever been claimed on the property...until recently.

According to the *Rebecca Nurse Homestead Newsletter*, an unusual event happened that is related in the Fall 2004 issue. One of the guides was giving a tour of the property. She was on the ground floor and sent the guests into the room ahead of her. When she arrived, she noticed that a cradle in the room was rocking and assumed that one of the visitors had pushed it. As she spoke about the room, a peculiar thing happened. The cradle did not slow down. Even as the group left, the cradle continued to rock. Eventually, it stopped (though, no time frame is given). Since that time, volunteers have made the cradle rock, to see how it moves when guided by human hands. And two things are clear: the only way to make the cradle rock is to push it...and the cradle only rocks for a short period of time, not nearly as long as it did that one unusual day. What could have caused the cradle movement? No one knows...perhaps it's a ghostly visitor that offers its own tours of the property.

Along with this, there are a few people who have reported taking pictures near the Rebecca Nurse memorial. On occasion, flashes of light and orbs have shown up on the pictures. Could it be just sunlight, casting an unusual shadow between the trees? Or, could it be a little bit more? Needless to say, the Rebecca Nurse home site is a unique piece of history that continues to evoke memories of the past.

Author's Note: The Rebecca Nurse Homestead is on Pine Street. Check their website for hours at http://www.rebeccanurse.org.

19

Danvers' Haunted Cemetery

Endicott Cemetery

The History

The old Endicott Cemetery on Needham Road (off Clinton Avenue) is one of those quintessential New England cemeteries. Located in a remote part of Danvers, it's a tiny cemetery dedicated to members of the Endicott family. This little burial ground neighbors a much larger burial ground known as Russell Cemetery, which is also difficult to find, and is a gentle reminder of the typical small cemeteries that dot many of the communities in the region.

A quick glance at the cemetery reveals an old collection of gravestones. Most of the gravestones have become rough with age and many are difficult to read. The online website *Geneaology Forum* provides an in-depth glimpse of the gravestones — as best they can be deciphered — and reveals that the cemetery was in use from 1750 to 1931. Almost every gravestone belongs to a person with the last name "Endicott" except for two that belong to members of the Hardy family, which married into the Endicott family, and one that belongs to the Maurice Ody, who also married into the Endicott family.

The gravestones belong to a wide range of Endicott family members, a family that dominated the region for many centuries and contributed to the history and growth of Danvers. Interned in this cemetery include John Endicott, an American army captain, and his family. Captain Samuel Endicott is also buried in the cemetery. He was descended from one of the original founders of

Salem who arrived on the shores of Massachusetts in 1628. A later John Endicott, who served in the Navy during World War I, is also buried in the cemetery.

The Mystery

Endicott Cemetery is one of the secret spots of Danvers. Even long time residents of the town have no clue where the cemetery is. Because it is secluded, visitors rarely venture into the cemetery, but it certainly is an ideal place for a ghost story.

According to several websites, this cemetery has been deemed haunted. Most stories report that three ghosts have been seen in the area. Typically, one of the ghosts appears to be a female, who is often accompanied by two smaller ghosts, which are believed to be children. The ghosts have been reported walking the small cemetery grounds, particularly at night. It's believed that the younger ghosts may be the children of the female ghost.

In one of those classic "truth is stranger than fiction moments," there is a little bit of irony in the cemetery. Most of the gravestones in this ancient burial ground have been toppled by time. However, three gravestones still remain. They belong to a woman named Margaret and her two sons, Alex and Jeremy. Coincidence? Hmmmm.

Adding to the unusualness of the Internet rumor is that there is a Margaret buried in the cemetery…but there is no record of an Alex or Jeremy buried there.

Now, curious, we checked this one out from afar. The cemetery itself is located on a stretch of land that is rather difficult to navigate. The original roads that led in and out of the cemetery have been taken over for commercial use and storefronts. However, from the mere looks of the museum, it looks quintessential Hollywood haunted. From a distance, all that can be seen of the old cemetery is a stone wall that stands out amid overgrown brush, shrubbery, and trees that themselves look like ghosts. Yet, despite the look of the place, we did not notice anything out of the ordinary when checking the cemetery from our vantage point. In fact, the cemetery looks like a peaceful place, which is surely what the Endicott family was striving for.

Part Three: Beverly

*B*everly is a large town bordering the Atlantic Ocean. First founded in 1626 as part of the city of Salem, the town eventually became its own settlement when founder Roger Conant broke with Massachusetts Governor John Endicott over religious differences.

Beverly evolved as a settlement that built its success on the ocean. Shipbuilding and fishing became important trades, supplemented by people who farmed in the area.

Beverly rose to national prominence in 1775 when George Washington arrived on the cozy shores. Realizing that the Patriot army's success hinged on a navy, Washington commissioned the schooner *Hannah* to be an armed schooner. From such humble beginnings, the first unofficial navy was born in America. The navy expanded and became official October 22, 1775, when the *Franklin* and *Hancock* became the first official ships to sail with the permission of the Continental Congress.

In the 1800s, Beverly evolved into a different type of community. Its close access to the ocean made it an ideal getaway for Boston's wealthy and prominent. For a time, it became known as a summer community. Yet, by the twentieth century, the town had evolved into a more industrialized city, with the revolutionary United Shoe Machinery Corporation dominating the landscape and bringing innovation to factory life. This strong company helped incorporate a rich work ethic into the city, which transcends to this day.

20

The Ghosts of Endicott College

The History

*I*n 1939, Dr. Eleanor Tupper devised a radical plan to address the growing needs of women of the day. Hoping to provide an opportunity for women to grow greater academically and professionally, she and her husband, Dr. George Bierkoe, founded Endicott College in Beverly.

From humble beginnings, a mighty college has grown. The original college consisted on a large estate purchased by Dr. Tupper and her husband. The first class graduated in 1941 with twenty female students. However, the college eventually grew in stature and students. As class sizes grew larger, the campus eventually spread along the pristine Beverly coast.

As time evolved, so did the mission of the college. The campus swelled to include more than two hundred acres of land — on which a beautiful campus has been built. The school, which served women for its first fifty-three years, became a co-educational institution in 1994. Offering a variety of programs and a notable leader in education, Endicott College has grown to a population of more than 1,500 students. It's one of the fastest growing colleges in the North Shore of Massachusetts.

The campus itself is a gem of a place. A compound consisting of old mansions, newer construction, a beautiful waterway, and oceanfront views, it is quite a site to behold. Students can go to class and then lie near the beach on late spring days. Alumni often flock for various functions at Tupper Hall — named for the founder — that offers beautiful views of the lush landscape in the region. Incidentally, it's a wonderful place to hold a wedding reception. In recent years, the campus has even built halls where visitors can spend the night.

The Mystery

As is the case with many colleges, Endicott College has provided fodder for several ghost stories that have been passed down through time. Often, these stories have been embellished and added onto as time progressed. Where the stories originated is hard to tell, but one thing is for sure…these stories have stood the test of time (the hardest test to pass in college).

Exactly what the nature of these stories is — fun stories to tell freshmen or interesting experiences that students have claimed to encounter — remains a fuzzy area. Even people who have attended the college are rarely certain of the details of the different stories that have evolved over the years. Here is a short collection of some of the stories that have become part of the Endicott legacy with a specific focus on the buildings that are haunted.

❖ **Brindle Hall** – This hall is a hotspot for supposed spectral activity. Different "unusual" events have occurred here, according to a many sources. Some students have claimed to hear banging on the headboards of their beds. When they ask for the noise to stop…the source of the noise typically complies. Handprints have been found to mysteriously appear on some windows…without a known cause. Window shades seem to pop up on their own…when rooms are uninhabited or when all the people in a room are accounted for (and of course, not opening the window shades). Strange sounds have also been known to echo through the hall, similar to that of whistling hot water kettle.

❖ **Reynolds Hall** – This hall was once a residence owned by Boston banker Herbert Mason Sears, who purchased the land called "Wood Rock" in 1907. As owner, he beautified the property with a lavish garden. The property was acquired by the Kendall family and made into the Kendall School for Girls. In 1939, the school was purchased as part of one of the original Endicott College buildings. The hall is believed to house the ghost of a young girl, perhaps even a student who attended the Kendall School—though no one knows who the girl might be. Window shades have been reported to go up on their own in the hall; piano music is sometimes heard

vemanating throughout the building, despite the fact that no one is playing music; and according to some sources, the image of a girl has been occasionally spotted in the mirrors inside the hall.

❖ **Winthrop Hall** – This hall is believed to be the former mansion of a sea captain who lived in the area. It's named for John Winthrop, the first governor of Massachusetts, and contains a lower level beneath the library that was used as a safe house for runaway slaves hoping to escape to Canada. It was originally called "Thissellwood," named for its original owner John Thissell, and was built in 1845. As told in a local legend, a woman dressed in blue and affectionately called "The Lady in Blue" (some people claim she is dressed in pink) has been seen wandering the area. Looking rather ghostly — which may seem obvious — she casts a heavy gaze to the sea. People who have witnessed her think that she might be waiting for her husband, who was lost at sea. Some people even speculate that she may have thrown herself to her death or hung herself in the house when she found out her husband had died at sea.

According to Sharon Love Cook, who attended the college and wrote the book *Real Life Stories of Supernatural Experiences* (edited by Ginnie Siena-Bivona), founder Dr. Tupper herself wrote that her daughter, Priscilla, claimed to have seen the Lady in Blue wandering the grounds of the college one day. Her daughter noted that, while she was walking, the ghost suddenly passed close to her. Clear in appearance, Priscilla soon knew she had seen something out of the ordinary when she realized the woman had *no legs*. The ghost is sometimes seen in the hall rearranging a painting in the foyer. She is particularly keen on turning it upside down — or at least she was in the 1980s.

❖ ❖ ❖ ❖ ❖

As you can see, Endicott College, like so many institutions, comes complete with its own ghosts. Whether or not these ghosts are real remains to be seen. Yet, they remain a special part of the local college lore to this day.

21

Old Time Haunts

The Ghosts of Beverly Cove

The History

*B*everly Cove is believed to be the oldest section of Beverly, a small city on the North Shore. The first settler arrived to this secluded bay area in 1630. That year, a man named William Woodbury constructed the cove's first house. More settlers arrived in 1636—the year the cove became an official settlement.

As time passed, the cove region grew. One of the more prominent families that lived in the area was the Lothrop family. Thomas Lothrop, who owned a large area of property in the cove, was the Captain of a company that fought in King Phillip's War, a large quarrel between Native Americans and the New England settlers. On September 16, 1675, Lothrop's men were lost in an attack in Deerfield, Massachusetts. The incident has been dubbed Lothrop's Massacre.

During the 1700s, Beverly Cove continued to grow. Several people from the region participated in the Revolutionary War. Shortly after the war, in 1804, the cove became home to a hospital servicing people with smallpox. To this day, the section is called Hospital Point.

By the early 1900s, the Cove was a popular tourist spot. Beaches, a tavern, and Stetson Cottage — known for hosting entertainers — made it a renowned stop in the region. In fact, President Taft rented out the cottage, and it was dubbed "the Summer White House," for a short period of time.

Beverly Cove is one of the oldest sections of Beverly. It's also considered the home of many old ghost stories.

In 1943, Lynch Park was opened in the Burgess Point section of Beverly Cove. It's a beautiful spot to visit with quaint gardens and ocean front views. It's also home to an amphitheater where local performances are held, helping to keep the memories alive.

The Mystery

However, the memories of a bit more linger in the area. Places that have since turned into private residences have become home to a variety of possible spirits. Some of the spirits are believed to date back hundreds of years.

According to author Lynda Lee Macken in *Haunted Salem and Beyond*, several ghosts were once spotted in homes in the area:

> ❖ The ghost of a young girl that is thought to have passed in front of a fireplace has been seen in at least one old home.
>
> ❖ A prankster ghost is thought to have patrolled houses, moving items from place to place.
>
> ❖ The ghost of an elderly woman has also been spotted in the Cove region. She actually has been located in rocking chairs, moving back and forth, as if trying to enter a restful state.

❖ A ghost has also been known to try to prevent the owner of a house from entering.

❖ And, according to Macken, there has been at least one incidence where water was found dripping throughout a house. However, when a plumber was called to resolve the situation, no source for the water could be found. The ghostly flooding eventually stopped.

Exactly who these ghosts might be remains relatively unknown. Perhaps they are early residents. Or, maybe they are victims from the Revolutionary War or Lothrop's Massacre. However, for a section of town rich in history, with houses that date back more than three hundred years, it's not surprising that some of the spirits might be trapped in the Cove. With the Cove's long history of fun and sense of community, it's easy to understand.

Author's Note: The ghosts probably inhabited land that at one time had public access, but now are private residences.

Part Four:
Marblehead

M arblehead is a breathtaking, historical city of the North Shore. Originally founded in 1629 as a fishing community, the city attracted a variety of stout-hearted and brave mariners from the coasts of England.

As Marblehead evolved, so did its seafaring reputation. People settled in the town just to participate in the lucrative fishing business that dominated the area. In time, sailors from the town participated in trade with the West Indies, bringing an influx of wealth into the area as well. By the early 1700s, Marblehead was one of the most important ports in New England. This mariner culture proved important to America during the Revolution as many Marblehead sailors, as part of John Glover's regiment, helped George Washington in his journey across the Delaware River.

Marblehead's success proved inconsistent following the Revolutionary War. With the advent of factory work and an intense development in shoe manufacturing, Marblehead slowly evolved into a shoe-making town. By the late 1800s, the town had gained prominence as a summer vacation spot — a title it still holds to this day.

Marblehead's rich tradition in American history proceeds itself and has been the source of some interesting, and chilling, stories.

22

Marblehead's Screaming Ghost

Screeching Lady Beach

The History

The residents of Marblehead have a long and proud tradition of turning to the sea. Throughout the past three centuries, the ocean has provided a way for people to make ends meet, been a resource for food, and been a quaint spot for recreation.

A quick tour around Marblehead reveals a charming town that has stood like a rock beside an unpredictable ocean. This ocean has churned out some major storms and powerful waves toward the rocky shore, but Marblehead has always withstood the pounding.

Small prominences and rocky inlets that cut into a craggy shoreline dominate the coastline of Marblehead. The geographic features have made the region difficult to navigate at times, but a splendid place for some unscrupulous characters to hang out.

It's believed that in the seventeenth and eighteenth centuries pirates roaming the oceans often made brief excursions to Marblehead to gather food and water, bury treasure, and, as the town and surrounding region become more populated, ransack villages for supplies. The town has several specific connections to pirates. A famous pirate named Jack Quelch frequented the town and eventually was captured by Boston officials near there. Snake Island, in Marblehead Harbor, was a popular spot for pirates to rest their ships and recover from chases at sea. At least one pirate ship is believed to have sailed from the harbor—a local ship that had been commandeered by pirates. One young man, Phillip Ashton, reportedly was kidnapped by French pirates and impressed into service. He escaped during a stopover in the Caribbean, hiding out in the local jungle, before returning home. Local lore also suggests that pirate treasure may still be hidden in portions of Marblehead — though no evidence has been found to substantiate such a claim.

Despite these connections to the past, it's one peculiar connection to the buccaneers of old that gives Marblehead more than its prosperous history. And so it goes... one fateful day, many years ago, pirates decided to make a brief stop at the town that, to this day, may still be remembered in a frightening way.

The Mystery

It's believed that sometime in the 1700s a pirate ship (thought to be from England, but perhaps from France) was patrolling the New England waters in an attempt to prey on English ships anchored off of Marblehead. The captain, squaring his spyglass on the salty waters surrounding the North Shore, spied a small Spanish vessel suitable for capturing. The seadog and his crew kept close watch over the unsuspecting schooner until twilight set upon the sea. As dusk turned to nightfall, and the pirates were certain that the mighty Marblehead fishing fleet had remained in the fishing grounds of the Grand Banks, a sinister plan unfolded.

The pirates pounced, sending their ship squarely at the Spanish vessel. Whether or not the men and women on board the schooner had a chance to escape remains lost to history. Chances are even if they had tried to move closer to land, the passengers would have had little opportunity to flee the onrushing pirates.

The pirates quickly overtook the vessel and boarded it. While they found the bounty of gold, silver, and jewels appealing, the pirates found the crew and passengers much to their disliking — mainly because they were witnesses to their act of piracy. The pirates did away with the passengers quickly...save one woman who bore a wonderful jeweled ring on her hand.

The woman was not particularly enthralled with the pirates. When the buccaneers demanded her ring, she refused. When they attempted to remove the ring, it would not budge. No one is quite sure what happened next. Some sources suggest that the pirates held onto the woman for a hefty ransom they

assumed would come from the husband of a woman wearing such a ring. Other sources suggest that the pirates took the woman immediately to shore as they accounted for their plunder. Either way, the pirates—and the woman—soon ended up on the shores of Marblehead, near Lovis Cove.

The residents in Marblehead took cover as soon as the pirates disembarked their ships, staying still in their homes as the pirates landed at the Cove and counted their stolen loot. While the pirates were gloating over the bounty, the woman made her way off through the night, hoping to find a sympathetic soul in Marblehead. However, before she could reach town, the pirates recaptured her. Angered by her attempt to escape, the pirates decided to get the ring once and for all. They tried to yank the ring off the woman. When this failed, they beat the woman on the beach.

Although her screams pierced the cool nighttime air, the residents in town were too scared to venture outside their houses for fear of the pirate retribution. The screams grew louder until at last...her voice was heard no more. Having killed the woman — and removed the ring, finger and all — the merciless crew returned to their ship and sailed away.

The following day, residents rushed to the beach to see what they could do for the woman. They found her dead, and quickly removed the body, giving it a proper burial.

However, the remnants of the vicious onslaught have not disappeared over the years. To this day, there are still reports of strange screaming in the nighttime air near Lovis Cove. The voice is strong and piercing — much like a storm gale — and is believed to be the haunting scream of the unfortunate woman killed many years ago on the shores of Marblehead. The screams are so vivid... that section of town has been dubbed "Screaming Woman Cove" and the beach itself is called "Screeching Lady Beach." According to author Pam Matthias Peterson in *Marblehead Myths, Legends, and Lore*, to this day there are people in Marblehead who refuse to wander the beach on a dark or foggy night.

23

Marblehead's Haunted Fort

Fort Sewall

The History

*P*irates and enemy ships. They were the scourge of the North Shore. Nowhere was this more present than in the village of Marblehead. Located in a prominent spot that jutted into Massachusetts Bay, Marblehead was vulnerable to quick attacks.

In 1644, the colony of Massachusetts decided to do something about that. They built a defensive structure — an early fort — at the site of Gale's Head in the town. Located on a rocky point that offered stiff protection, the fort would provide the security that the village needed against anyone who would do it harm.

The fort played an important role throughout the history of the village. During the seventeenth century, it helped keep pirates at bay. In 1742, additional defenses were added to the fort to provide protection against French ships that would often visit the area during the French and English conflicts. Townsfolk added to the fort during war times, and it was further restructured in the late 1700s, as a barracks and storage place for weapons and gunpowder. The fort was used during the War of 1812, offering protection from the British ships that patrolled the New England waters. It's noteworthy for being a place of shelter during one tumultuous chase involving the *U.S.S. Constitution*. On April 3, 1814, Old Ironsides used the soldiers stationed at the fort for protection from two British ships that were in hot pursuit, hoping to sink the dreaded U.S. battleship. Toward the end of the war, the fort was officially named Fort Sewall, in honor of Judge Samuel

Sewall, a prominent member of town. Sewall became a justice for the Massachusetts Supreme Court.

The fort remained active during the Civil War. In 1892, the United States government deeded the fort and land to the town of Marblehead. Over time, it has been developed as a park, with beautiful views of the surrounding North Shore region. The fort is also the site of Glover's Marblehead regiment. This is a group of Revolutionary War re-enactors who depict life in the fort at the time of the Revolution. Glover's regiment helped navigate Washington's troops across the icy river during the famous Crossing of the Delaware. Today, the fort is still used as a popular spot for people to visit. It also contains some of the old underground rooms and quarters that are off limits to the public, having been long sealed for safety reasons.

The Mystery

The old fort may not just be a remnant of a bygone era. In fact, it may *hold* some remnants from a bygone era as well. In the summer of 2008, Nicholas Smith, who runs Crypto Paranormal Investigations (CPI), got permission to do a preliminary investigation of the area. According to a *Salem News* article written by Allen Burke, Smith, a

New York native, has been a summer visitor to the region and knows some of the historic places quite well.

CPI, like many investigative crews, tries to use scientific equipment to rule out paranormal activity in potentially haunted sites. According to the article, Smith, using a tape recorder, found some rather unusual activity during a routine check of the fort. Smith did a simple countdown of readings, calling out "point-one," "point two," and so on. All seemed normal with little background noise—until he played the recording back. Following "point-four" on the recording, Smith says that a type of Electronic Voice Phenomenon (EVP) can be heard in the background asking, "What is point-four?" Because the fort had few, if any visitors at the time, Smith found the reading intriguing.

Following the unusual EVP recordings, Smith later went back to see if he could locate a source for the recorded voice using a more sophisticated microphone. He asked a series of questions, to hopefully flush out the potential cause of the noise, particularly if it had a paranormal source. While recording the answers, he again found an EVP, which seemed to shout "help" or "help me" several times. Along with this, the sounds of smashing glass seemed to also be heard in the background.

In an email, Smith says that it's difficult to determine why hauntings occur in any place, but often a lingering feeling can be the cause. While he knows of no deaths at Fort Sewall, he does suggest there is reason to believe prisoners were held in the barracks of the fort. Such trauma, combined with "an atmosphere of order and repetition, as they would have been prevalent at a military barracks, would set up a situation that MIGHT be conducive for a haunting to be formed."

At the time he began researching the fort, Smith did not even think the fort would be a site for paranormal activity, as he had never heard of any hauntings occurring there. He conducted his research as more of an exercise and was surprised to find that EVPs appeared on his recordings. Smith says the EVPs were some of the best audio evidence his organization has recorded. And, although he would still like to do work at the site, he believes he has collected enough evidence to think that the site is haunted, adding it's "a label I give to very few sights."

The mystery of Fort Sewall remains unsolved for now. Were the whispers that Smith recorded a sign that ghostly activity permeates the walls of the fort? Perhaps. And it might make sense. According to records, the fort was used to house prisoners in the past, particularly during the War of 1812. Some of the conditions that existed at the fort were believed to be less than pleasant and unclean. So, the ghost might just be a former prisoner hoping to break the bonds that once shackled him or her to the fort.

Part Five:
Gloucester

No other city in Massachusetts epitomizes the strength and spirit of the maritime trade than the city of Gloucester. Forever intertwined with famous fishing fleets, Gloucester is a city that was built by the ocean.

Samuel de Champlain was one of the first Europeans to visit Gloucester, coming ashore in 1606. John Smith of Jamestown fame explored the region as well, paving the way for English settlers. In 1623, members of the Plymouth colony visited the area for the nearby codfish. They caught fish and used the shores to dry the fish. This paved the way for settlers to arrive in the mid 1600s.

Gloucester began as a fishing community, but the settlers also made a living farming. However, in the 1700s, the abundance of trees in the area made Gloucester a sailing capital of the thirteen colonies. Ships were built from these trees and soon the Gloucester ships were famed throughout the world. During the next 150 years, Gloucester built a sturdy reputation by the sea, its ships gaining prominence throughout the world.

The maritime culture is still an important part of Gloucester. Fishing fleets still sail from the city, as they have done for centuries. At the same time, the city has become a popular spot for visitors, artists, and celebrities alike...making it easy to understand why the city has many interesting stories to tell.

24

Gloucester's Ghost Town

The Legend of Dogtown

The History

hile the name may not seem glamorous at first, Dogtown, Massachusetts is actually the nickname of a long abandoned portion of Gloucester that was originally called "The Commons Settlement."

The settlement was established along the nexus of the North Shore at the time. It was a thriving community, dependent on trade and agriculture, established along the main roads that led to all the towns of Massachusetts's Cape Ann. Between 1650 and 1750, the town thrived, and many of Gloucester's most famous families lived in this section of town, with residents making a living farming, lumbering, and building transportation.

The town began a steady decline in the 1750s, as the landscape of New England changed with the events that led to the Revolutionary War. A few of the residents in the town gained local fame for their antics during the Revolution, including a man named Peter Lurvey, who noticed the arrival of a British warship in the Gloucester harbor and encouraged local residents to launch an attack on the ship. The attack was a resounding success, causing the British to leave the harbor. Despite the success, Lurvey succumbed to injuries suffered in the battle and died. Another resident, Isaac Dade, was impressed as a sailor on a British warship at the age of eighteen and later escaped. He joined the American army and fought valiantly in the culminating battle of the war at Yorktown.

Despite such important moments, the Commons continued a downward spiral. The lack of forests, the end of piracy in New England — which led many people to seek shelter inland from the Gloucester shore in the first place, and eventual war with England caused people to abandon the town by the late 1700s. Once the United States won its freedom from England, people no longer needed to be sheltered from pirates and British warships. And with it the need for the Common's settlement diminished.

Following the war, many families moved to the Gloucester shore, where the success of the fishing and shipping trade proved a strong lure. Families who had staked their claim to the shore prior to the American Revolution seemed to do quite well here, so many of the "commoners" joined them. However, a few of the seafaring families refused to leave their beloved homes, so a small settlement remained established for some time. As time progressed, the settlement slowly diminished as sailors who had lived in the beloved town went out to sea and never returned. The remainder of the settlement included the widows of these sailors, or widows who lost their husbands during the Revolution. These widows, seeking safety, would purchase dogs to help protect the homes. When the widows died, the dogs roamed the streets of the town on their own, forming small packs that searched for food. Eventually, the town was nicknamed Dogtown because of this.

As the last of the main families died off, another class of residents took shelter in the slowly disintegrating town. People who were homeless, needy, or hoped to prey on the few travelers who passed nearby took shelter in the abandoned and slowly dilapidated residences. What these newcomers could not garner from travelers, they gathered from the landscape around them. They typically subsisted on wild berries, fish, squirrels, and other fowl that they could obtain. Countless stories, legends, and tales have been told about these people — in particular two women, who were considered witches, left a particularly interesting reputation on the land — and the spirit of Dogtown lingers to this day in the imaginations of old New Englanders.

Eventually, the last resident of Dogtown was forcibly removed from town in 1830. Nicknamed "Black Neil," the man had performed odd jobs for the transient residents of the town in the early 1800s. When all of the remaining residents had left or died, Neil took up residence in the abandoned shell of a house, living off the land as best he could. When he was found in 1830, he was taken to a poorhouse, where the food and quality of life

was better. Unfortunately, the sole survivor of Dogtown died a week later.

Dogtown lingered in obscurity for some time. There was fleeting fame when a man named James Merry declared that, even though he was sixty years old, he could outwrestle a bull. Merry had done this in the past and wanted to show the world, or at least Gloucester, that he could do it again. He decided to prove it by holding a wrestling match in the old vicinity of Dogtown. Alas, the bout proved to be much like a modern-day match, with the heavyweight bull being too much for the lightweight man—Merry succumbed to injuries suffered during the bout.

Dogtown would probably have disappeared into the dust of old library books if it had not been for a man named Roger Babson. The founder of Babson College and a Gloucester resident, Babson decided to bring a little spark to the old village once and for all. The land of Dogtown had become known well for its large rocks and some very interesting boulder formations. So Babson mapped trails of the old town and even numbered the ancient foundations of the old houses, which can still be seen today. During the height of the depression, he hired unemployed stonecutters to carve inspirational messages into the sides of twenty-four large stones, which remain along the trails that run through the old town. Even today, the Dogtown Advisory Committee helps to ensure that the old town is protected from development and maintains the upkeep of the old land as a testimony to Gloucester's unique past.

The Mystery

Any town that has disappeared into the past is bound to have a few interesting stories to it and Dogtown is no exception. Many of the people who took up residence in the town during is waning years have become the subject of local legends.

Perhaps no two residents of the old town are more renown than Judith Rhines and Tammy Younger, the two women who considered themselves the "Witches of Dogtown." Both of these women tempted men in their own way in hopes of gaining material goods in some form or another.

Rhines was a younger temptress who was always on the prowl for a sailor who happened to be passing by. As soon as she spotted a young man that sought her fancy, she often put on her Sunday—or perhaps Saturday—best and rushed off to meet him. Often, she would convince the sailor to spend time with her in exchange for goods or other money to help her get by.

Tammy Younger, ironically the older witch of Dogtown, performed her "witchly" duties in quite a different way. Instead of searching for men, she would often wait for them to find her. A behemoth of a woman, who allegedly had teeth that resembled tusks (an unfortunate accident performed by the local barber and amateur dentist who tried to pull her teeth to no avail), Younger typically scared away local folk. However, her talent for telling the future seemed to gain her much acclaim from local pirates, sea farers, and privateers who moored their ships near Dogtown just to have the chance to speak with Younger and have their fortunes told.

For those who passed close to the Younger estate and failed to check in, a special type of doom overcame them. It was believed that Younger and a similar "witch," Luce George, would stop anyone who failed to visit with a simple gaze. Their look could stop a carriage in its track — so it was said — and Younger and George (sounds like an old gangster group) would often procure goods from the carriage before allowing it to continue along.

However, not all of the Dogtown residents were quite like this. There was a lady named Becky Rich, who made her fame from brewing a unique blend of plants and herbs to make a saucy beverage known as Dire's Drink. People would come to Rich's home just to purchase the beverage, which had a knack for curing colds. The customers would often linger for dinner, where she would invariably tell their fortune.

Another person who lived in town was Sammy Markey. He originally made his way as a housekeeping peddler, offering washing and ironing duties to those who lived in the area. However, as the town began to change, so did his duties. Later in life, he turned to coffee as a means to survive. And his unique talent with coffee? He used the grounds to predict the future.

And so it was that Dogtown became the prognosticator's alley, where pirates and wary travelers alike would pass time, sometimes unintentionally, until the last person left in 1830.

Dogtown remained in obscurity until Babson attempted to map the area and turn it into an inspirational spot in the 1920s and 1930s. To this day, people visit and listen to the ancient words of wisdom on boulders as they winnow their way through the decaying remains of the old common houses.

Yet, it isn't just these words of wisdom that some people hear. There are a few who suggest strange and elusive voices can be

heard in the still air surrounding Dogtown on quiet days when the winds are hushed. Voices that have echoed the sands of time... Voices that seem to have no origin...except in the past. The voices, sometimes vague whispers that might be telling a fortune or the voice of a privateer seeking a bit of food, often mix with a bold energy that people feel as they meander through the ruins. These voices are believed to be the ghosts of the old Dogtown residents, stuck in time, reminiscing about days in the past...and perhaps seeking a new passerby to enchant with tales and fortune telling.

Babson Rock Quotes

In the 1920s, Roger Babson purchased the land once known as Dogtown and helped open it to the public. He created a WPA job program on the site, employing people to chisel his favorite mottos into the large boulders on the once vast glacial moraine. The result is a natural "instruction book" that everyone can enjoy:

❖ Be clean	❖ Be on time/study
❖ Courage	❖ DT SQ (Dogtown Square)
❖ Get a job	❖ Help Mother
❖ Ideals	❖ Ideas
❖ If work stops, values decay	❖ Industry
❖ Initiative	❖ Integrity
❖ Intelligence	❖ Keep out of debt
❖ Kindness	❖ Loyalty
❖ Moraine	❖ Never try, Never win
❖ Prosperity follows service	❖ Save
❖ Spiritual Power	❖ To Rockport
❖ Truth	❖ Work

25

Gloucester's Famous Monster

The Sea Monster of the North Shore

The History

Since the time of the first European visitors to North America, the North Shore of Massachusetts has been a staple of maritime culture. By name alone, the "North Shore" shows that a certain degree of the populace subsisted on maritime economy. And, indeed, the North Shores' history is intertwined with the ocean.

Gloucester is well known as a fishing seaport throughout the country. Fishing boats leave the port daily to cast their lines for the treasured fish that once used to teem off the waters of Massachusetts. Long days, harsh weather, and pounding waves mark the lives of those who live in the often-idyllic seaside village.

Salem, to another extreme, made its money through the international shipping trade. Once one of the most important port cities in America, Salem garnered fame for its trade with Asia, not its witch trials. Sailors, captains, and merchants alike made money from the famous China Trade that permeated the landscape during the early nineteenth century.

And Beverly, an often forgotten sea town, brought a different maritime fame to the area. Drive through the town and you will be sure to see signs proclaiming that Beverly is "the home to the American navy." Washington's meager force, which was predominantly privateers, anchored off the Beverly shores during the early days of the American Revolution, protecting the shorelines from British warships that preyed on unsuspecting villagers.

With a rich maritime culture, there is little doubt to the reason why so much ocean-bound folklore abounds in the area. From war heroes, to famous shipwrecks, to tales of ships that went to strange lands, the North Shore has its own rich maritime traditions. But, one of the most interesting folktales involved a series of sightings that have persisted until modern times of a strange animal found off the shores of Cape Ann. Tales of this strange sea creature, often called the "Gloucester Sea Monster," have challenged the mind, inspired the imagination, and added to the lush heritage of the North Shore.

The Mystery

The first mention of a sea serpent off the coast of Massachusetts dates back more than three centuries. In 1639, John Josselyn, a visitor to the New England shores, reported a story he heard regarding a sea serpent in Cape Ann. Josselyn mentioned that the serpent was often seen lying on Cape Ann rocks. Josselyn got his information secondhand. According to the story, a boat carrying two Native Americans and English fishermen passed near the creature, but when the fishermen suggest shooting the creature, the Native Americans explained that a failed attempt might have fatal consequences.

The most celebrated sighting of the sea serpent occurred in 1817. During that year, the serpent was spotted numerous times in the waters around Gloucester, often passing close to ships in the harbor. The serpent appearances started simply enough, with a brief sighting on August 6 of that year. Two women and a swimmer were near the water's edge when a strange object appeared in the water. At first, it looked like nothing more than a shadow, but then it became apparent that the object looked like a creature.

The first sighting brought little more than a few chuckles and some raised eyebrow. But August 6 would prove to be NO joke. As the month progressed, more people saw it. The creature swam past ships. It appeared before numerous members of town. Citizens, who were well respected, such as clergy and judges, reported seeing the strange creature in the water. The sightings were met with skepticism in many scientific circles, but brought flocks of people to the town in hopes to see the strange serpent.

David Humphreys, a respected general and former member of George Washington's staff, was so awed by the reports that he decided to investigate. He arrived on the scene and began to gather eyewitness testimony. According to his research, as well as reports in *The Boston Messenger*, a newspaper at the time, the sea serpent ranged from sixty to seventy feet long. It had a head larger than a dog's and was similar in shape to a turtle's. It appeared to have a foot long horn, similar to a spear, protruding from its head. Its body was equivalent to the width of a barrel and it moved around in snake-like fashion, easily able to turn at a moment's notice.

Although the creature remained elusive, the emergence of such an unusual species caused great excitement in the community. Several fishermen stepped forward to corroborate the initial reports of the creature. On August 14, a shipmaster named Solomon Allen III said that he had seen the creature for three straight days. The following day about two-dozen people reported seeing the creature playing off shore.

While there were many sightings, a fair amount of the populace doubted that such a creature existed. Despite such doubts, the reports of the creature persisted for some time. Soon, a $5,000 reward was posted for the creature. A few hunters ventured in the water in hopes to net or even shoot the creature. However, the creature was too sly, evading any attempt to stop or capture it.

On August 18, 1817, the scientific organization known as the Linnaean Society of New England began its own investigation of the creature. Due to the efforts of a local man named Lonson Nash, the testimony of eight witnesses was used to gather a composite of the creature. Witnesses disagreed on its appearance — some said it was black, others noted it was brown; some thought the creature looked like buoys while others referred to the body as "cask"-like. Even the length of the creature varied. However, it became apparent that all eight witnesses, who had frequented the water, believed that the creature was something they had never seen before. After gathering information and sorting through the reports, the society decided that an entirely new type of creature had been discovered, though they still were not certain what it was.

The serpent made various appearances off the shore of Gloucester for the remainder of the year. In September 1817, a sea captain in Rockport, Massachusetts claimed to have killed a giant snake in the water that stretched nearly three feet long. Some people believe that the snake might have been the progeny of the Gloucester sea serpent. The Linnean Society eventually obtained this creature and studied it; linking it to the Gloucester sea serpent, they declared that overwhelming evidence made them conclude that a new genus had been discovered. They quickly dubbed it *Scoliophis Atlanticus* (or Atlantic Humped Snake).

The news was not widely embraced. In fact many scientists had their doubts about the creature, and when it was later discovered that the Linnean Society's specimen was in fact a misshapen terrestrial snake, the doubters of the Gloucester sea serpent emerged in full force. Some people thought the reports were simply a publicity stunt drummed up to bring visitors to Gloucester. Others believed the publicity of the sea serpent caused more people to think they had seen such a creature as well.

The following summer, the serpent supposedly reemerged off the coast of Maine and Massachusetts. It was spotted in Portland Harbor and near Salem during the months of June and July. In mid August, it appeared in Ipswich Bay, prompting a local whaling captain named Richard Rich to track it down. After a two week search, all that Rich was able to find was a rather large blue fin tuna. Although he declared this to be his monster, many doubt that he actually mistook the tuna for the creature and simply wanted to return with something. This made many skeptics wonder if the sea serpent was actually a misidentified creature.

During the summer of 1819, the serpent made the last of its spectacular returns to the area. In June, it was spotted by a schooner passing close to Cape Ann. As the summer progressed, reports of the serpent surfaced throughout Massachusetts, with sightings occurring in many places including Scituate and Boston. Finally, toward the end of summer, the serpent found the waters near Nahant to its particular liking. Hundreds of people reported sighting the sea creature in the shores off the causeway-linked town. More people rushed to the town to catch a glimpse of the famous creature.

However, as quickly as the serpent arrived, it disappeared — after 1819, reports of the creature are fewer and far between. In fact, it would appear almost as if the creature had totally left the New England region for, perhaps, better feeding areas, much like migrating whales do during a change in season.

In 1822, the sea serpent emerged again in Nahant. According to reports, the creature appeared every day during the summer. The serpent took a brief respite from the Massachusetts waters until 1826, when it returned on a similarly daily basis in the waters off the coast. The serpent also made regular visits to the region in 1833, 1834, and 1835.

According to author and New England sea serpent researcher J. P. O'Neill, reports of the sea serpent were sporadic after the mid 1800s. In the article "The Great New England Sea Serpent," O'Neill mentions that many of the sightings would have been forgotten if not for the work of a Gloucester resident named George Woodbury, who kept a personal scrapbook of sea serpent sightings. Woodbury's book shows that the sea serpent again reappeared in 1844 off the coast of Marblehead, as it suddenly raised its head out of the water, surprising two children who were breaking the Sabbath law with a Sunday sail.

Woodbury's scrapbook contains other anecdotes as well. Supposedly, the creature reappeared in 1878, off the coast of Plum Island. There, several children watched a serpent-like creature swim off the shore before it disappeared.

Another gem in Woodbury's scrapbook suggests that a fishing crew ran into the serpent, or another one like it, not too far from the coast of Boston. The crew of the ship *Philomena* encountered the serpent entangled in its nets. While trying to remove the serpent, the crew ended up in a fierce, "Jules Vernes-esque" battle, as the men tried to tug the net and its load back out to sea. With the help of two other ships, the men were eventually able to subdue and kill the creature, which they said was about sixty feet long, as round as a large tree trunk with black skin covered in barnacles. The captain of the ship, a man named McKinnon, regrettably cut the serpent loose after the battle, but acknowledged that his and other ship crews had seen the serpent—affectionately called Big Ben—during the past twenty years.

Woodbury's last account places a similar creature, perhaps a relative of Big Ben, near Cape Ann in 1914. There, each crewmember of the British schooner *Flora M* witnessed a snake-like creature emerge from the depths of the Massachusetts Bay. The head resembled that of the horse as the creature moved quickly, disappearing under the ship and resurfacing ahead of it before disappearing altogether. Was it possible that yet another creature survived?

Whatever was sighted in the waters off of Massachusetts remains unknown. Yet, to this day, the story of the Gloucester Sea Monster makes people wonder what exactly lives off the coast of the North Shore.

North Shore Sea Serpent Sightings

❖ **1639, Cape Ann**: John Josselyn hears a tale about a sea serpent that rests on the rocks in Cape Ann. He's told that fishermen and boaters are encouraged not to shoot it for fear that the creature might attack.

❖ **1817, Gloucester**: Famous sightings of the creature bring hordes of people to Gloucester, particularly in the summer. The Linnean Society of New England announces that the sea serpent represents a new genus of creature. This new genus is later discovered to be a land snake.

The famous Gloucester Sea Monster made some of its most memorable appearances along the Nahant shoreline, seen here.

❖ **1818, Salem, Massachusetts and Portland, Maine**: A sea serpent is again spotted. Captain Richard Rich (not to be confused with the comic book character) attempts to capture the serpent, but fails.

❖ **1819, Nahant**: A sea serpent, perhaps related to the Gloucester creature sightings, is spotted. Mobs of people flock to town in hopes to spy the serpent. Large interest in sea serpents is sparked in America.

❖ **1822, Nahant**: A sea serpent is regularly seen, nearly everyday in the summer.

❖ **1826, Massachusetts**: The sea serpent reappears off the coast.

❖ **1833-1835, Cape Ann**: Reports of the sea creature resurface.

❖ **1844, Marblehead**: Two boys report seeing a serpent's head emerge off the shore.

❖ **1876, Plum Island**: Children and one adult witness a serpent swimming in the waters off shore.

❖ **1912, Massachusetts Bay**: Crewmembers of the *Philomena* and two other ships engage in a fierce battle with what appears to be a serpent like creature in its net. The creature succumbs to wounds suffered in the battle and is released.

❖ **1914, Cape Ann**: Crewmembers of the *Flora M* all report seeing a serpent in the waters off Massachusetts.

26

Gloucester's Haunted Castle

Hammond Castle

The History

*J*ohn Hays Hammond Jr. was an interesting man. Inspired by the invention and creativity of Thomas Edison, Hammond dedicated his life to inventions. He formed a company — the Hammond Research Company — that proved highly successful. Hammond and his company helped to develop four hundred patents and the ideas for twice as many inventions. While you might not have heard of Hammond, you probably can thank him for some of his important research…especially if you love television: Hammond proved particularly interested in studying radio waves and is often dubbed the "Father of Remote Control." Now, how many of you are impressed!

In 1926, construction began on a unique house for the Hammond family. Intended to house the Hammonds, as well as their business, the structure was a magnificent mansion lying in the tranquil village of Gloucester near the ocean seashore. The house took three years to build and the result was a magnificent castle that resembled the medieval structures of yore. Hammond loved the house and used it to store a variety of artifacts and antiques he had collected. Hammond had a keen interest in the medieval period, as evidenced by pieces in his collection.

The Hammond Castle has existed since the late 1920s and now serves as a popular tourist attraction for visitors to the North Shore. People can tour the castle and visit various rooms, including a library, a war room, an invention room, a kitchen, and at least two bedrooms. Hammond also built a network of secret passageways into the castle, to add to the mystery of the building. Of course, Hammond had a keen sense for recreation, and included an indoor pool into his final design. Many of the artifacts that Hammond collected are also still located in the castle. This includes a screen that Johann Sebastian Bach supposedly played behind, a treasure chest (without the treasure of course), and — some people claim — a skull the belonged to a member of Christopher Columbus's crew.

Hammond lived in the castle until his death in 1965. Supposedly, he is buried on the grounds with his deceased pet cat. Sound interesting? Well, Hammond was certainly an interesting man. Local lore suggests that he asked for his tomb to be covered with poison ivy so no one would bother him in the afterlife. Some people speculate that Hammond had a desire to return to the world reincarnated as a cat. When a black cat showed up at the castle some time after his death, and often was seen resting in Hammond's favorite chair, more than a few eyebrows were raised. Some thought it might be the original owner himself, returning from the dead.

The Castle hosts a variety of special events throughout the year. It's also home to one of the most spectacular Haunted House tours around Halloween; one the locals say is a "can't miss" attraction.

The Mystery

Like any medieval-type castle, what would Hammond Castle be without a few ghost stories—and Hammond Castle indeed has a few.

According to popular lore, the ghost of Mrs. Hammond is believed to haunt the castle. Her ghost has been spotted in several places in the building, including one of the bedrooms. She has also been located on the balcony and is often spotted near an organ.

Strange noises have been heard and shadowy shapes have been seen throughout the castle. Sometimes, the noises come from furniture that has been moved. Other times, it comes from voices that are heard to permeate the section called the Tower Galleries. However, they are not just ordinary voices…they are voices that speak in different languages. Along with the voices, odd shadows have been cast along the walls and halls of the castle. Those who heartily believe that ghosts inhabit the castle suggest the multicultural display of ghostliness comes from lingering spirits attached to Hammond's artifacts.

Some people believe that Hammond's pet cat haunts the grounds as well. Hammond did have several cats (scratches from their claws can still be seen on some furniture inside the castle) and some ghost fans believe that at least one ghost cat prowls the castle. Strange scratching sounds have been heard on the property, which lend credence to these stories.

Others have reported that Hammond still wanders the house and property…and no longer as a cat. According to some sources, Hammond was a firm believer in Spiritualism. Perhaps he may have found a way to return from the dead or maybe he is looking for one more invention to work on.

The castle may also have an energy spot that attracts different types of spiritual energy. Hammond was such a believer in the ability to contact the dead that he may have conducted such experiments inside his home using a Faraday cage. The purpose of this device, used in electrical experiments, was to contain energy. It was hoped that the cage would allow spiritual energy in and funnel it toward a medium. How this cage may have worked is no longer known; however, some people speculate that a light spot found on the floor in the main hall is a result of these experiments—and some people claim that there is residual spiritual energy in the castle as a result of this experimentation.

Several other ghosts are also believed to inhabit the house. In fact, it seems to act like a hot spot of paranormal activity for some people who have reported seeing ghosts in the house. No one knows for sure why the house — if it is haunted — has so many haunts. But some people have theorized that Hammond collected so many items from around the world that spirits and energy associated with these objects have congregated at the Hammond Castle. Which leaves no doubt that the Hammond Castle, like most medieval structures, has some interesting history to it.

Part Six:
Essex

$\mathcal{E}$ ssex is a small, charming town located near the extremity of Massachusett's North Shore. Once a part of Ipswich as an area known as Chebacco Parish, Essex broke off to form its own town in 1819.

Once established, Essex built a reputation as a shipbuilding community and, according to some people, the shipyards built as many as 5,000 ships, including many used in Gloucester's famous fishing fleet.

As time evolved, the importance of Essex as a shipbuilding community changed. The town took on a new look, eventually becoming a quaint lure for people interested in touring the North Shore. Essex has several eating establishments, stores, and antique shops. It also has a long history as part of the fabric of Massachusetts—and, as with many places, it has its own interesting stories as well.

Essex's Phantom Eater:

The Ghost of Windward Grill

The History

Windward Grille, 109 Eastern Avenue, is the name of a quaint restaurant located in this historic seaport. The grill is situated in a house that is at least three hundred years old. Originally built on land given to Deacon Burnham as payment for his services in the Pequot War — one of the early wars between Native Americans and the colonists in New England — this house has certainly withstood the test of time.

The house was passed down through generations of Burnhams until 1897. According to an article appearing in *The Gloucester Times*, some local residents believe that the farmhouse served as a station on the Underground Railroad and may have held a safe house in the upstairs attic. Eventually, the house came into private ownership and, by the twentieth century, had been converted into a restaurant. Before it became the Windward Grille in 2004, the restaurant was under other ownership and called the Hearthside.

The Mystery

While the Windward Grille appears to be a typical restaurant situated in a house that has been affected by time, there seems to be something unearthly that has also affected the former farmhouse. Apparently, a ghost of some sort may have taken up residence in the restaurant.

According to the newspaper article, many workers at the former Hearthside and current Windward Grille have experienced many unusual things in the old house. Staff members have reported seeing:

- knives *float* in the air;
- shadowy figures roaming the halls;
- toilets flush under their own devices;

❖ lights flicker;

❖ tables becoming mysteriously stuck in place, unable to move

Sudden changes in temperature are also the norm in this restaurant.

One of the more unusual experiences actually happened several times when the restaurant was the Hearthside. A couple, believed to be in their 30s, was spotted *materializing out of a wall* in the dining room, often floating in the air. The woman appeared to be decked out in a long, white dress, as if attending a formal affair. On other occasions, a different woman, with dark hair, also sporting a dress, is seen at the top of stairs.

The strange events have not been relegated to inside the restaurant. In October 2007, there was evidence to suggest that — maybe — one of the ghosts decided to venture outside the house. This unusual event occurred on a moonlit night when two cars were driving in opposite directions near the restaurant. Without warning, a woman appeared in the middle of the street, waving to the drivers, as if signaling them for help. Surprised, the two drivers swerved to avoid the woman and provide assistance. The cars collided, resulting in an accident. Yet, the drivers were probably unconcerned about their cars at first. They were more worried about the woman...that is, until they found that the woman had somehow, strangely, disappeared. Instead, there was an injured rabbit in the middle of the road. The rabbit hobbled off as quickly as it could.

Who was the woman? No one is too sure. She vanished a little too quickly before anyone could find out. Perhaps she was indeed a kind Samaritan helping an injured animal that quickly ran off after the accident. Or, as others believe, she was a benevolent ghost who happened to arrive on the scene to rescue an animal.

Whatever the cause, the Windward Grille appears to be a "can't miss" restaurant for any would-be ghost hunter.

Part Seven:
Newburyport

*N*ewburyport is a section of the North Shore located at the mouth of the Merrimack River. Originally settled by Pawtucket Native Americans, European colonists arrived in the 1630s to establish a settlement.

Newburyport slowly grew into a prosperous community. Initially divided into two sections — the fishing port section and an agricultural interior section — the two eventually split into two separate towns. Newburyport became a fishing community, while Newbury residents pursued farming interests. Newburyport residents saw tremendous success during and shortly after the Revolutionary War period. An economic downturn hurt the community after the War of 1812, and slowly the town evolved into an industrial city.

By the late twentieth century, Newburyport transformed itself into a charming town known for its stores, parks, and boardwalk. It's a can't miss tourist attraction that draws many visitors every year.

27
Newburyport's Tall Tale

The Haunted Schoolhouse
of Charles Street

Having visited Charles Street, we can indeed say that the school no longer exists as it once did. The school may be one of the private residences on the street...or it might have been built over long ago (it's difficult to tell). There is no sign to mark the former schoolhouse. However, having wandered down the street and spent a little time on the sidewalks, there is certainly no eerie feeling or presence associated with the street. In fact, it appears to be a quaint street filled with apartments and houses that reflect the old-town charm that continues to exist in Newburyport. But who doesn't like a good tale, so read on...

The History

Newburyport is a quaint sea town along the North Shore of Massachusetts. Known for its seafood shops and pretty views, Newburyport seems to hardly be the type of town that would have a dark secret, particularly one that would raise eyebrows throughout town. However, in the 1870s, the town apparently had a ghost problem.

The problem began at the Charles Street School for Boys. A school that had been built at least two decades before, it was well known in the community. It seemed like your simple one-room schoolhouse for the day: neat, clean, and uncomplicated. It had four windows on each side, a basement, and was in a slightly deteriorating condition, but nothing seemed out of the ordinary...except the fact that the school was a slight eyesore in a rather pleasant, well-kept neighborhood.

And then...*something* strange arrived.

The Mystery

In the 1870s, when Lucy Perkins served as teacher there, a series of unusual events began to rock the school. Out of the blue one day, the school seemed to be victim to a prank. Strange knocks permeated from the floorboards of the schoolhouse during morning prayers. The knocks traveled across the room, resting near the desk at the front of the room. The following day, the same thing happened. Soon, the knocking was a regular occurrence. The knocks would persist throughout the day, interrupting student recitations and occasionally reverberating off the door. Sound like a childish prank? Well, it was more than just a simple April Fool's joke.

Other strange events occurred as well. The bell on Perkin's desk would ring on its own. The lid on the stove that warmed the room would lift into the air, float, and then return. Children's coats would be cast to the ground. Dustpans and brushes hanging on walls were flung to the ground. Doors would open. A large ventilation shaft in the school, which had probably rusted with age and hardly budged, opened often by itself.

At first, Miss Perkins kept the details of the events quiet. She assumed it was a student causing problems. She often tried to find the culprit, rushing to doors and checking the grounds for the cause of the noise, to know avail. Fearing that the cause might be unexplainable and perhaps supernatural, Perkins decided to tell the school committee. But, they were hardly receptive until — and this part of the story is not quite as well known and is subject to debate — a strange boy started appearing at the school.

The boy was unknown to Perkins or the children in the school. He had a forlorn look in his crystal blue eyes. His skin was pale and he wore brown clothes that had long gone out of style. He gazed into the window during the day, almost clamoring to come in. It's reported that, on occasion, his arm appeared in the middle of the classroom, hovering in the air. Was there a lonely

A long view of Charles Street. This street is home to one of North Shore's most famous ghost stories...but was it all a hoax?

ghost hoping to go to school? Perhaps that was a really clever child who was utilizing his own precocious magic? Or, was their something more sinister occurring? Soon, the town heard of the events, and the school committee was forced to act.

News of the events spread. Newspapers carried the story. Parents began taking their children out of the school. The caretaker of the school refused to enter the building alone.

As the story of the bewitched schoolhouse was told and retold, stranger things continued to happen. The stove would move overnight. On windy days, when thunderclouds cast a dark shadow, a strange yellow glow would fill the room.

Townsfolk became worried. Who—or what—was invading their local school? Some residents wanted to close the school and demolish it. Others hoped to investigate the events. It's believed that Oliver Wendell Holmes even became involved in the investigation. Would anyone ever get to the bottom of the events?

To this day, no one knows exactly what happened at the Charles Street Schoolhouse. After investigating, Holmes apparently became convinced that the paranormal activity was hardly paranormal at all. In fact, he believed it had a rather ordinary cause — a mischievous lad. However, at the time, no student came forward to claim responsibility for the ghostly events.

What was the source of the trouble? No one really knows.

According to local legend, the school had been the site of an unfortunate event sometime in the 1850s or 1860s. One of the local boys had acted inappropriately at school. As was customary for the day, the boy received a typical beating and was kept in the basement for the remainder of the school day. When school ended, the boy was released and allowed to go home. Supposedly, he died later that night. Many people, at the time, believed that the boy had decided never to leave the school again.

As suddenly as the events started, they stopped even quicker. In 1875, the events simply came to an end. The case seemed closed. Why? It has been stated that séances were held to ease the former student out of the school and into a new resting place.

Yet, the true story is lost to history. Most of what we know about the events comes from two published stories called *Expose of Newburyport Eccentricities, Witches and Witchcraft,* published by someone named H. P. in 1873, and *The Haunted School-House at Newburyport, Mass* published the same year by Loring Publishing in Boston—but another, perhaps more likely, twist to the tale surfaced years later. Two different people claimed to be involved in creating the ghostly disturbances in the schoolhouse. The first was a student named Amos Currier whom, some believed, was originally discovered by Holmes as the cause of the hoax. Although he denied involvement in the ghostly story as a lad, he did later admit to being part of the hoax. Another man named Edward De Lancy claimed to have perpetrated the hoax. He explained that he had owned a machine that could trap light and another machine that tossed objects. De Lancy used them regularly near the school.

To this day, no one really knows what happened at the Charles Street School. While some people claim it was inhabited by a supernatural spirit trapped in time, others held firmly to the idea that the ghost was no ghost at all...just a good practical joker. Since 1875, the "ghost" has never returned. However, despite its sad condition, the schoolhouse remained opened. It eventually became a private residence and may still exist as one to this day. And, no one has ever reported the slightest hint of a ghost, eerie lights, or strange sounds...except maybe for the wind that blows against the roof during a cold northeaster.

28

Where Every Ghost Knows Your Name

David's Tavern

The History

*B*etween 1806 and 1810, Moses Brown built the Brown Square House. Brown, who had been born in West Newbury sixty-four years earlier, learned the carriage business as a lad and developed a business to manufacture these vehicles. Finding it profitable, Brown amassed a small fortune prior to the Revolutionary War and invested his money in the rum and molasses industry. Following the war, he opened a rum distillery in Newburyport in 1792. Brown's reputation and fortune grew, and soon he was scooping up nearby property, eventually purchasing land for his own house that was built in the early 1800s.

A merchant, landowner, and shipbuilder by profession, Brown certainly could afford building a large house. Build it he did! For years, Brown's house was a well-regarded spectacle of Newburyport. A reflection of the wealth and prosperity of Newbury at the time, the Brown Square House served, at least in part, as Brown's private residence for more than twenty years, until his death in 1827. However, as the times changed and America became embroiled in the War of 1812, hard times hit. America entered a depression and Brown's business tailed off. He began renting out portions of his residence to business owners.

Following Brown's death, Sarah White Banister, his only living heir, came into the property and eventually turned it into a boarding house by the mid-1800s. The building remained a boarding house until 1879, when the Brown Square House became a hotel. The following year, after Banister's death, the hotel officially became dubbed the Brown Square Inn—and an institution was born. The hotel offered lodging to visitors and was updated in 1907 to include indoor plumbing, heat, and electricity. In 1922, the hotel was sold and opened a year later as the Garrison Inn, in honor of Newbury resident and abolitionist William Lloyd Garrison, whose voice, determination, and skill as a speaker were instrumental in the fight to end slavery.

Today, the Garrison Inn remains as a reminder of the past while continuing to serve as a hotel to this day. It is part of the National Landmark Registry. The Inn, dubbed "Boutique Hotel," contains twenty-four rooms and modern amenities. The hotel is also the home of a restaurant called David's Tavern.

The Mystery

While the Brown Square Inn might be known for its place in history, it's also known for being the location of a potential haunting, as many people say that more than one ghost is believed to haunt the inn property and David's Tavern.

In an article from the *Daily News of Newburyport*, the idea that ghosts might be haunting the inn and tavern began to surface in the early 1980s, when the Brown Square Building was renovated and refurbished as part of the inn. With major renovations, some of which unveiled the building's long-covered charm, the Garrison Inn opened for business in 1982. According to the article, bartender David Tarr said that at the time of the opening, the haunting-type incidents were simple and easy to recognize...including smashed windows that appeared without cause.

But, as time went on, the ghostly appearances have evolved into something a little bit more. In the article, Tarr and manager Chris Gissel say that the ghosts have developed other ways to show their possible presence during the last twenty years. They include:

❖ Objects have been seen falling off shelves.

❖ Staff members have felt mysterious taps.

❖ Sudden cold spots occurring in the tavern.

❖ Shadowy figures have been seen in places that were otherwise unoccupied.

❖ Candles have been spotted moving around tables.

Some people have even claimed to spot a woman, believed to be Bannister, and a tall man wandering through the tavern and into the inn.

According to an email from Shannah Hiatt, who has worked at the tavern for ten years, the stories about the ghost sightings have seemed to diminish recently. However, she did offer a few thoughts about the sightings. Hiatt explained that one of the incidents involved a housekeeper working in the lobby. She went into a closet and then moments later *bursted out* the closet and the hotel, believing that someone or something had touched her in the closet.

Hiatt also related two other incidents in which she was personally involved. Once, she recalled being in the tavern and suddenly hearing her name called. She turned around and saw no one there. Hiatt believes there may have been a natural reason for the occurrence, but it still causes her to pause and think about the mysteries of the restaurant. On another occasion, Hiatt felt someone approaching her from behind. Although she did not feel threatened by the energy, she went into defense mode. She assumed a friend was trying to scare her.

"When I felt like they were within inches of me, I turned around to see who it was," she wrote, "but, wow, there was no one there."

Hiatt doesn't know if there are any ghosts in the tavern, but these two incidents have left her wondering.

The hauntings have come and gone with no apparent purpose, but it appears that the ghosts might have checked into the inn and the bar to stay. Whatever their reason for spending time in the bar, the staff believes that the spirits are friendly and enjoy their visits, no matter the time of year.

The Garrison Inn and David's Tavern are part of the long time landmark known as Brown Square. They are also the site of a series of possible ghost sightings.

29

The Strange Creature of Newburyport

Massachusetts' Bigfoot Sighting

The History

Plum Island is a small barrier island found in the North Shore. Comprising parts of four surrounding towns — primarily Newbury and Newburyport — the island is a hot spot for visitors who come for a variety of reasons. Tourists and residents alike relish in the scenery, the animals, and the quiet solitude found on the island. Separated from the mainland by Parker River, a portion of the much larger Merrimac River, one can easily see why Plum Island is a popular stopover.

The island is named for the dominant feature of its landscape known as plum bushes. These bushes grow a small plum fruit that is used in cooking and baking. The bushes cover the island and lend a lavender hue to the landscape upon harvest.

The island is known for two other main attractions. The first are the beach areas that offer a tempting invitation to residents and visitors alike. They provide a welcome respite to all visitors on warm, summer days. The beaches abut several properties, from quaint summer cottages to large mansions. Such properties are found throughout the island, making it a charming place.

Along with having beaches, the island is home to a wildlife center known as the Parker River National Wildlife Refuge. Found on the southern section of the island, the 4,600-acre site is far from the more settled northern section. The refuge provides a home for more than 350 species of wildlife, including the piping plover (a federally protected bird). It opened in 1942 to serve as a protected area for migratory birds that passed through the region. Several small habitats abound in the area, including a salt marsh, a beach area, bogs, mudflats and, according to the Friends of Parker River Wildlife Refuge website, one of the last remaining untouched "dune complexes," in the northeastern part of the United States. The refuge includes trails, decks, and observations towers that allow visitors to see some of the most pristine views in the region. Visitors are allowed to drive through parts of the refuge and can use a long boardwalk to see other parts of it.

The Mystery

While the refuge may be home to a variety of known species, it may also have been the home to one rather unusual—and cryptic—species. According to the Bigfoot Field Researchers Organization and the Gulf Coast Bigfoot Research Organization websites, the Parker River refuge, or at the very least the abutting roads, may have been the spot of a possible Bigfoot sighting.

According to the websites, the potential sighting of the hairy creature occurred April 13, 1978. Two visitors to the park had stopped to enjoy one of the park's views with their children. They went to an observation tower near the Pine Trail area section of the park. While enjoying the scenic vistas of the spring day, a series of strange noises caught their attention. The noises started out as simple clicks and then turned into more of a high-pitched scream.

Because there were no birds or other animals visible in the area, the visitors decided to leave. As they reached their car and started to leave the refuge, a shadowy figure emerged from the greenery that borders the road. For a brief moment, the strange creature crossed the road to enter the marshy area. The report mentions that the creature was large — about seven feet tall — with lanky arms. It lumbered in a forward tilting gait as it crossed the road. It had dark hair, or at least a black coloring, and disappeared quickly into the woods. As drivers passed by the spot where the creature had crossed the road and entered the woods, they paused for a moment, but saw nothing. The strange creature had disappeared.

Was this the first case of the Plum Island Bigfoot sighting? Was it another type of unusual creature? Or, perhaps there is some other explanation for the strange occurrence that day. No one can be too sure. However, there have been other reported Bigfoot sightings in the North Shore area, including one in the town of North Andover. There are are also many more reports of the creature throughout New England. So, it's not out of the realm of possibility that, if there is indeed a Bigfoot that once visited Plum Island, it might have been there like any other traveler. Perhaps it was out for a stroll, or simply enjoying the scenery. What better place for such a creature to do it than at the federally protected refuge on Plum Island.

10 *Clues That You Have Found A "Bigfoot"*

Chances are that you will never have a Bigfoot encounter, but...on the rare chance that you might be caught off guard by a large, hairy creature, how can you be sure that the Bigfoot you see isn't a guy in a gorilla costume? Or someone who hasn't shaved in a while? Well, based on several sources, here are ten signs that you may have found a Bigfoot.

1. **Giant footprints** – Now, we're not talking about a Shaq O'Neal size 100 here. This is one of those honest to goodness footprints that sticks out like a sore thumb and looks like the type made by a big (possibly hairy) man.

2. **Hair** – Of course, many animals leave this behind, but if you find some hairs that look like they belong to a rather large bear, you might just have found a Bigfoot. Researchers, who claimed to have found a Bigfoot hair, report they are coarse and much like that of a bear. But...be aware that, if you *do* find such a hair, the source may also be a rather large bear. So proceed with extreme caution.

3. **Broken twigs** – Sure, it goes without saying. Sasquatch isn't blazing a trail. Just by walking through the woods, this big guy is bound to break a lot of low lying branches, bending them in the direction that he's walking. But...*do not* be too excited if you see this, as other animals do this, too.

4. **Handprints** – You might also find handprints of a Bigfoot. While considered less common than other evidence, the handprints typically look wider than a human with short fingers and, some people believe, a thumbprint that suggests that Bigfoot lacks an opposable thumb.

5. **Bigfoot scat** – Believe it or not, like most animals, Bigfoot has to go the bathroom at some point in time. They typically leave scat behind, which you may encounter. Sometimes, you might be lucky, or unlucky as the case may be, and run into a scat pile twenty inches long or more. This could be a sign of a Bigfoot...or just as possible, another animal in distress who overate and now feels a great sense of relief. Incidentally, if you look through the scat (not a recommended activity unless you know what you're doing), you might find remnants of leaves, small animal bones, and seeds.

6. Sounds – Occasionally, people have allegedly heard the "scream" of a Bigfoot in the woods. Now, unless something unusual is going on — you never know what might happen in the woods — and the sound has no known source, keep your ears and eyes open. The scream is so unique that expert woodsmen and woods women do not know what type of animal is making it. However, other sounds have been linked to the Bigfoot as well, including grunts, moans, whistles, and howls… that could mean it might communicate like most animals.

7. Bigfoot nest – If you wander into a stretch of woods and found a weird lean-to, be aware that it might not be the local scouts in the area. Some Bigfoot investigators have reported finding Bigfoot nests. They often resemble a crude lean-to or wigman-like structure that was made quickly. These shelters might just belong to a Bigfoot…or perhaps someone who was temporarily lost in the woods.

8. A really bad smell – If you happen to encounter a really strange smell in the woods (not attributed to the fact that you or fellow campers might not have bathed in a week), be aware that a Bigfoot might be in the area. Some reports of Bigfoot sightings suggest that the creatures often leave behind a rather pungent scent. The scent has been compared to the smell of an overflowing diaper pail, with enough power to be felt for nearly one hundred feet. Perhaps this is Bigfoot's kind way of saying, "Don't mess with me!" Or, it might actually be a plant, like a skunk cabbage, that you just stepped on — another reason to watch where you step in the woods.

9. Clacking sticks – Perhaps you have heard of the old gag that clacking two sticks or rocks together will keep away predators in the woods. Well, the Bigfoot might have heard of this rumor as well. According to some enthusiasts, Bigfoot might bang rocks or sticks together as a form of communication. So, if you encounter any strange banging sounds watch out, it might just be a Bigfoot (or, worse yet, a landslide).

10. Big, hairy guy – I know it sounds odd, but most people who report seeing a Bigfoot see a big, hairy creature that looks like a tall, and often slender, ape. Unless a zoo is nearby, you might just have found your Bigfoot.

30

Newburyport's Haunted Graveyard

The Ghosts of Oak Hill Cemetery

The History

O n July 21, 1842, Newburyport established the Oak Hill Cemetery. Also known as State Street Cemetery and located on a large (at one time, four acres) parcel of land at State and Parker streets, the well maintained graveyard is one of the largest in Newburyport and — as graveyards go — is definitely a historic stop.

While Newburyport might seem to be a quiet suburb north of Boston, it holds its own fair share of history and the Oak Hill Cemetery pays tribute to this history, as several notable residents have been interred here. According to the website "Gravematters," which documents graveyards throughout the country, the Oak Hill Cemetery is the final resting place for politicians, religious leaders, and other celebrities. Notable people who have been interred here include:

❖ **Moses Brown**. This merchant, who died in 1827, was one of the wealthiest men in Newburyport. He owned a rum distillery and eventually established Brown Square House, which currently houses the Garrison Inn…a site also considered haunted.

❖ **Frederick Strong Moseley**. A philanthropist who once owned many acres in Newburyport, he died in 1935. His land has since become Maudslay State Park.

❖ **Donald McKay**. A ship architect and boat yard owner in Boston, McKay died in 1880. He is known for designing many of the Yankee clipper ships in the mid-1800s. McKay's design set sailing speed records and helped revolutionize American trade throughout the world.

❖ **Harriet Elizabeth Prescott Spofford**. This writer, who died in 1921, was a renowned author of her day. Known for dabbling in gothic romances and mysteries, her books often challenged female stereotypes.

❖ **Elissa Landi Thomas**. This actress, who died in 1948, starred in several motion pictures, including "The Count of Monte Cristo" (1934). She was also known for writing poems and was the author of six novels.

❖ **William Wheelwright**. This industrialist, who died in 1873, had a variety of business interests in Central America and South America. They include a trade route across Panama and a steamer and railroad route in South America.

The Mystery

While Oak Hill Cemetery may hold its share of history, it also holds a little bit of intrigue as well. According to several Internet sites, Oak Hill Cemetery is home to a variety of unusual, some say even *supernatural*, events. These events reportedly include a homeless woman who used to sleep in the cemetery, a tombstone that suggests a person might have died while eating a pea, and a potential spot of a murder, or so says some local urban legends.

According to the "TheShadowlands" website, which highlights incidents of hauntings, the cemetery is believed to be the site of some strange doings. Some people who have visited the cemetery have reported being overcome by a strange feeling as they enter the cemetery. These reports suggest that something intangible— perhaps a ghost or a strong presence—overcomes the people as they enter the cemetery grounds, nearly overpowering them. It has been suggested that this temporary condition might be due to ghosts trying to scare visitors away. The cemetery has also been the site of vandalism in recent years. Perhaps, because of these events, spirits of the cemetery have a reason for keeping visitors at bay.

A post on *My UFO Blog: Haunted Places in Massachusetts*, reported that the cemetery might also be the site where a family was murdered. The spirits of these ghosts have not left the cemetery and seem particularly interested in protecting it. Four ghosts have been spotted in the cemetery, particularly at night, chasing any visitors away. According to the blog, they seem to be interested in keeping the cemetery safe from any intruders at night — friendly or not so — and are believed to be the ghosts that overpower some visitors to the cemetery.

The source of this story — and the potential source of the strong presence — remains unknown. But there is no doubt that that Oak Hill Cemetery, in Newburyport, is certainly a final resting spot that is hardly your typical burial ground.

31

Newburyport's
Haunted State Park

An Urban Legend:

Beautiful Maudslay State Park

The History

*I*n the late 1800s, Frederick Strong Moseley was a well-known man in Newbury. A stockbroker (called "note broker" in the day) by trade, Moseley made a fortune and a philanthropist reputation by the end of the nineteenth century.

In the 1890s, Moseley purchased 480 acres of land in Newburyport and developed a large estate that remains to this day. Employing the services of architect William Rantoul, landscape architect Martha Brookes Hutcheson, and horticulturalist Charles Sprague Sargeant, the Maudesleigh estate was built during a fifteen-year period between 1895 and 1910 on the banks of the Merrimack River.

Over time, Maudesleigh evolved into a truly remarkable estate. It consisted of a main house with seventy-two rooms, surrounded by houses for a gardener and a forester, a large pool, and three

According to a current urban legend, Maudslay State Park may be haunted by strange spirits. Does this peaceful state park hide a secret history?

greenhouses. Numerous gardens dotted the land, including a two-acre vegetable garden, fruit trees, a perennial border garden, a rose garden, and an Italian garden. A second large house was built between 1939 and 1941 to accommodate Helen Moseley, Frederick's daughter.

At its pinnacle, Maudesleigh was supervised by forty staff members and boasted an impressive array of flora. Yet, over the last half of the twentieth century, conditions on the estate deteriorated. The main house was razed in 1955. The smaller house, built for Helen Moseley, was gutted by fire in 1978. The grounds became difficult to manage and the Maudesleigh of old began to vanish.

In 1985, the Massachusetts Department of Environmental Management acquired the property and slowly turned it into the Maudslay State Park. Although most of the buildings have disappeared over time, some of the early structures are still visible. Old stone bridges and paved roads remain in the park. The upper foundations of the main house still can be seen in parts of the grass, when mowed. The greenhouses, pool, and many of the gardens still exist to some degree, but are in poor shape.

The park itself is in rather good shape, however, and is one of the forgotten gems of the North Shore. According to the official website, the park offers an ideal place for recreation. The views of natural mountain laurel and rhododendrons are a site to behold, particularly in late spring. The park also has bike paths, horseback riding trails, and hiking trails that can be used by visitors who choose not to take part in the guided tours that are offered by the park service. There are places to walk or go cross-country skiing in winter. Maudslay State Park also hosts several events throughout the year. One of the more popular events takes place near Halloween. The local theater group that performs in the park, the Theater in the Open, hosts a "Maudslay is Haunted" event, complete with short skits, scary stories, and haunted attractions. Restrooms are available on site and visitors can walk the grounds even in winter (though some trails are closed due to the fact that they are near bald eagle nests). Admission is free, but there is a parking fee.

The Mystery

While tourists comprise the bulk of visitors to Maudslay State Park, there are some people who claim this park is sometimes host to other "visitors." These visitors, believed to be supernatural, lead some to believe that Maudslay is haunted more than just at Halloween.

According to several websites, Maudslay State Park has long held a reputation as a haunted spot. Many ghosts have been spotted in the park, and other unusual events have been attributed to the park as well.

One of the posts on the "TheShadowlands" website highlights the haunting history of this park. The poster, who grew up near the park, explains that local lore suggests unusual events have been happening in the area since the 1600s. People believe that witches once used the lands as a gathering spot. While such evidence is hard to prove, New Englanders in the seventeenth century did believe that witches gathered in central, wooded locations, similar to those found in the park.

The writer of the post also suggests that other legends abound about Maudslay, including the possibility of hidden tunnels, shape shifting trees, and strange auras. While most of these stories sound like pure fiction, the writer, like others who have visited the area, have mentioned the presence of auras and other colors amid the shady pine trees at night. Likewise, some visitors to the park have mentioned feeling a strange uneasiness overcoming them...as if they were being watched or were not welcomed to the area.

Having visited a portion of the park, it was hard to feel any uneasiness. It's quaint, quiet, and well maintained. It is also quite an inviting park that lends itself to a weekday or weekend family outing.

Perhaps these feelings are just coincidental, either nature at work or the effect of the park's densely forested landscape. Or, they might be the result of something unknown. Whatever the source of the strange vibes, there are many who believe that Maudslay State Park is not only haunted by the Theater in the Open at their annual fundraiser, but by real spirits who lurk in the park and apparently do not want others to visit.

Part Eight: Nahant

$\mathcal{N}$ ahant is a picturesque community found along the rocky shores of northeast Massachusetts. Known for its famous causeway that connects the community to the mainland, Nahant is a favorite tourist spot during the summer.

In 1640, a small population of fishermen began to call Nahant home. By the mid 1600s, the town became farmland for Lynn. Wood was cleared and the land was tilled for crops.

Over time, Nahant became a popular escape for surrounding residents. Hotels and summerhouses dotted the landscape and soon... the small town was a resort.

Nahant continues to maintain this resort nature to this day. While the town includes several residences, its tourist charm is evident in every turn. Along with this charm, are some interesting stories that survive to this day.

32

The Haunted Island of Nahant

The Legend of Egg Rock

The History

Roughly a couple of miles off Lynn Beach in Massachusetts is a small granite island that rests like a lone statue in the middle of the Atlantic Ocean. Facing a constant pounding by the relentless sea, Egg Rock has been a dominant feature in the New England landscape for centuries.

First dubbed Bird's Egg Rock because of the numerous birds' nests that once dominated the landscape, the small island is about 200 feet wide, 750 feet long, and 80 feet above sea level. The stoic island has withstood the test of time, becoming a durable statement about the venerable New England shore. This durability has led the island to become an important feature of the North Shore coast.

Egg Rock first came into prominence as the site of a lighthouse constructed in 1855. The lighthouse was designed to help local sailors, particularly those of Swampscott, reach the nearby shores safely. The lighthouse proved a valuable resource, illuminating the North Shore skies until 1922. Its importance as a nightly landmark was evidenced in 1897, when the structure was burnt by fire and quickly rebuilt

While the lighthouse served an important purpose for ships in the region, there was one significant drawback. The rock itself has no suitable landing spot for ships. Any boats that hoped to seek shelter on the island during a storm risked running ashore

This is a view of Egg Island from the Nahant Shore. The bird sanctuary is also the supposed home of a long lost ghost.

on the craggy shores. Local residents rectified this problem in 1906 with the construction of a landing stage on the island.

In 1922, the lighthouse became inactive. It was sold to a private owner that year. However, the lighthouse seemed to have a mind of its own. In the midst of transporting the lighthouse off the island, it slid off its staging and fell into the sea, succumbing to the rocky waters that it helped to protect. Without a lighthouse, Egg Rock slipped into a more docile past time, becoming an official bird sanctuary in the mid 1900s.

The Mystery

Egg Rock holds a special place in the hearts of Nahant residents. The local island is subject to a variety of interesting tales that have stood the test of time. Perhaps the most popular story is that of a dog named Milo, who belonged to the first lighthouse keeper, a man named George Taylor. Milo took his job of lighthouse dog seriously. During stormy days and fog-ridden afternoons, Milo would often take to the shores, barking out at will like a four-legged foghorn warning any sailors passing by that they were close to the isle's rocky shores. According to

legend, Milo also rescued several children who became stranded in the rocks surrounding the island. The story of Milo became so well known that the dog became a national celebrity in the mid-nineteenth century. His tale was spread throughout the country.

However, Milo isn't the only legend of the island to survive to this time. A local story tells of a second lighthouse keeper named Thomas Widger, whose wife was pregnant with their third child. On the day that she was to give birth, Widger rowed to shore in the midst of a brewing storm. He arrived in Nahant, seeking a midwife to help deliver the child. When the midwife saw the festering storm beginning to rage in full fury, she opted not to join Widger, fearing that the stormy waters would capsize his rowboat and be the end of all of them. A lesser man might have agreed and stayed safely ashore instead of facing a raging nor'easter, but there was no way Widger was going to leave his wife alone. He rowed through the storm, cutting across waves and fighting piercing wind in order to arrive at the lighthouse. He made it to the spot just in time to help his wife deliver the child.

Yet, perhaps the most interesting story of Egg Rock that still exists to this day involved a strange tale that predates the lighthouse and one that still may have relevance. According to local lore, an Italian immigrant named Faustino rowed from Nahant to Egg Rock one day in 1815 in hopes of gathering flowers for his fiancée, a woman named Alice. After roaming the island, collecting his own bouquet, he made his way to a rowboat and began to row back to Nahant. A sudden wave struck his rowboat, knocking him into the cold Atlantic Ocean. Perhaps

caught in an undertow or perhaps unable to swim, Faustino never made it back to shore. He drowned in the cool waters that same day.

However, Faustino might not be lost to history. People who have visited the island, or even gazed at it from shore, have reported hearing the name "Faustino" echoing in the air around the island. According to those reports, the voice calling in the night belongs to that of a woman, believed to be Alice, whose ghost never left the world. Apparently, she may still visit Egg Rock from time to time, searching for any sign of her former beau.

33

Nahant's Witch Cave

The Secret Behind Swallow Cave

The History

The year was 1675 and New England was in the midst of a fierce battle. Because of politics, tensions over hunting grounds, and misunderstandings, a war erupted between colonists and the surrounding Native Americans. Led by King Phillip, the Native Americans joined forces against New England colonists. The result was a series of attacks called King Phillip's War, where towns and Native American villages were destroyed.

The war had a major impact on the New England region. Since the Pilgrim's first arrival at Plymouth, settlers had lived in relative peace with Native Americans in the region. However, by the 1670s, that relationship had soured. Colonists' need for land and a series of problems between Native Americans and settlers turned the tide on the relationship.

Tensions boiled when the colonists captured Wamsuta (also known as Alexander), son of the chief Massasoit, who had brokered peace with the original Pilgrims of Plymouth. The colonists hoped to question Wamsuta about his intentions, but he died while in their custody. His death sparked resentment from the Native Americans. When Alexander's brother, Metacom (sometimes called Metacomet), took his brother's place, he decided to take a more aggressive approach to the colonists in Massachusetts. Instead of seeking peace, Metacom, known as King Phillip to the colonists, tried to form a confederation of Native American tribes. He hoped this union would launch a war against the colonists and send them from the shores of

New England. Soon enough, King Phillip's War erupted throughout New England, and nearly every town in the region became embroiled in the war in one form or another.

The war lasted a year, culminating in the death of King Phillip in the swampy lands of Bridgewater, Massachusetts. The colonists were able to defeat the Native Americans and decided to come down with a heavy hand — fist really — on most tribes in the area. The colonists forced many Native Americans out of their lands and into harsh conditions on surrounding islands and lands, essentially ending the Native American way of life in New England. An unfortunate aspect to the war is that many of the tribes were loyal to the colonists and even assisted their cause during the war; yet, despite the loyalty, the colonists effectively chased the tribes from the region.

The Mystery

Several mysteries surround King Phillip's War, many of which are part of the local fabric of New England. But, perhaps none are as interesting, and more forgotten, than the story of Swallows Cave in Lynn.

The cave itself has evolved over centuries' worth of battles with the ocean. The fierce tide no doubt has left its mark on the roughly chiseled cave located near the Northeastern University Marine Lab in the coastal town. The cave, named for the abundant flock of birds, notably swallows, that once inhabited the landmark, is hard to find and seems hewn from the solid granite coast.

The cave's role in the King Phillip's War is as much folklore as it is conjecture, but according to the stories written and passed down through the centuries, it marked one of the more unique twists in the war. The cave first came into prominence in 1675, when a band of Native Americans, siding with King Phillip, decided to attack the important coastal community of Lynn. More than three-dozen warriors rowed on canoes from Cape Cod, crossing Massachusetts Bay, arriving on the rocky shores of town. There, they infiltrated the village, attacking in a quick burst of fury.

It did not take long for the Lynn colonists to realize who had attacked. Like they did in so many other towns at the time, King Phillip's allies raided Lynn. The colonists grabbed muskets and repelled the attack. The Native Americans retreated to the surrounding town of Nahant. Running across the rocky cliffs, they opted to remain in the region, regroup, and launch another assault on the town.

While the Lynn colonists gave chase, they managed to lose the band of Native Americans. Perhaps, finding their canoes, or perhaps scanning the ocean and realizing they had not left the region, the Lynn settlers became wary. They feared another attack and began preparing for a return visit.

Several community members decided to thwart their attack. A group of men left town and headed toward Salem. They searched the town for a woman named Witch Wonderful, who had an uncanny power to predict the future. As soon as they entered Salem, they found the witch, but did not have to speak a word. She explained to the visitors that she understood why they had come, and that she knew where the Native Americans were. She told them that the Native Americans planned to attack the town again and were hiding in a cave in current day Nahant.

Grateful, the Lynn visitors returned to town and told fellow community members about the information they had gleaned. Then, a small group of armed men embarked on a preventative strike of their own. They left town and went straight to Nahant. There, they scrambled across the craggy shore and soon discovered the Native American hideout.

Poised to attack, the Lynn volunteers waited for the right moment. Then, when it appeared the moment had come, a stranger appeared out of nowhere to interrupt the battle. It was none other than Witch Wonderful who walked up to the defacto Lynn commander. She warned him not to attack or shed blood on the spot. Instead, Wonderful explained that she might be able to convince the Native Americans to surrender.

No doubt amazed by the woman's abilities, the Lynn men agreed. Wonderful climbed down the rocks, descended into the cave, and disappeared. Soon after, she emerged with the Native American group, who agreed to surrender to the Lynn men. The Lynn contingent in turn agreed to help the Native Americans return to Cape Cod as a condition of their surrender.

The Lynn townspeople were pleased with Wonderful's assistance. In the intervening days, Wonderful offered another prediction... she would die in a matter of weeks. And, within two weeks of the attack, she did pass away. In honor of her deeds, the people of Lynn claimed Wonderful's body and buried her on a small cliff overlooking the cave.

Wonderful's place in New England lore was firmly established at the time of her death. However, what makes the story even more unusual is that Wonderful might still be leaving her mark on New

England, for there are many people who have claimed to see Witch Wonderful still scaling the cliff tops or even walking through the cave in Nahant. Other people claim to see a woman dancing along the cliffs. And still others claimed to have heard odd voices and unusual singing in the area. A few even say that more than one figure has been seen haunting the spot. Although such reports are sporadic, they have occurred for more than three hundred years. Who might it be? Perhaps it is Wonderful, just making another visit to the cave.

There is an interesting ironic side note to this story. When you think about it, the fact that the settlers went to a person who claimed to be a Salem witch in the first place is amazing. At the time, there was nothing wrong with such an occurrence. Settlers often accepted the fact that witches lived in New England. Although the behavior was not condoned, nothing often happened to supposed witches like Wonderful. However, just seventeen years later, her skills would have been deemed unacceptable when the Salem Witch Trials occurred — proof that times indeed change quickly even in the late 1600s.

Part Nine:
Lynn

ynn is a large city in Massachusetts that has played a pivotal role in the commerce of the commonwealth. Originally founded in 1629 by Salem residents who hoped to find more room to grow, the first settlement came from land purchased from the Saugus Native Americans by the English colonists who founded a community in the North Shore. The land became various present-day towns and cities, including Lynn.

Lynn garners its name from a city in England. The first settlers made their living off the land and in the ocean. Over time, though, Lynn developed from a rural farming area to one of the industrialized capitals of Massachusetts in the 1800s. Known for its shoe industry, and later its business industry, Lynn has kept the pulse of local economics.

Industry aside, Lynn also gave rise to several important components of local and American history. It was the site of Frederick Douglass's first public speech. It was the site of a revolutionary way to manufacture shoes. And, it's the home to the first jet engine, manufactured at the General Electric factory in 1941.

Lynn has played an important role behind the scenes of Massachusetts. As part of this role, a little bit of history still lingers in the town.

The Legend of Dungeon Rock

The History

The mid 1600s was a dangerous time for people living in New England. With Native American tribes providing a danger from the east and French settlers offering an equal danger from the north, there were few outlets to turn for safety. And, when pirates began arriving at the shores of New England at the same time, there was certainly reason for fear and hesitation throughout the land.

The year 1658 turned out to be one of those years, as a strange ship arrived on the eastern horizon and made its way to Massachusetts's North Shore. The ship was a dark black color and bore no flags — a sure sign to the wary New Englanders that this was no ship to tempt. As people on the North Shore watched the ship in one part angst and one part fear, they noticed that it slowly made its way toward the Saugus River.

As soon as the ship anchored near the river and a boat was lowered, carrying a small crew of four people, the surrounding folk were put on alert. They knew the worst. These strangers seemed slightly familiar...and if that was the case, it meant only one thing: Pirates!

The strangers traveled down the river with something in tow, arriving at a spot near the present-day Saugus Iron Works. The spot, which to this day is still referred to as Pirate's Glen, was a temporary holdover. Once there, the pirates secretly made a deal with a local blacksmith. Leaving behind a note, the four visitors suggested that they would leave some pieces of silver at the smith's shop in exchange for some tools.

Knowing it was wise not to anger such "quiet" visitors, the blacksmith obliged and left the tools at a pre-arranged secret location. The visitors than took the tools, walked deep into what are now the Lynn woods, and found a natural cave. Inside the cave, they got to work, and quickly completed their task — hiding what is believed to be a large quantity of buried treasure.

Soon after the arrival of the buccaneers, a British warship arrived on the horizon. It had been seeking out pirates and, when the ship neared the Massachusetts's coast, the English crew soon learned that a pirate ship had moored nearby. Now, the main pirate ship probably had left the area as soon as it had seen the British ship cross the horizon, but the British didn't mind. All they were concerned about was the notion that — according to some local townsfolk — a few of the pirates were still on land.

The British got to work right away. They went down to the river and began traversing the woods in search of any peculiar fellow who looked a might bit out of place. History has clouded the exact details, but it does record one thing — three of the pirates were found. One proved to be a man named Captain Harris, who was the commander of the ship. However, the other two have been lost to history. Some people claim that the two were women, who were traveling with the captain; others say there were two other pirates. Whatever the truth is, the British captured the pirates and, under British law, there was only one thing to do with pirates — execute them. So, the British soon returned to their homeland with three pirates, who were later hanged.

Yet, one pirate remained behind. A man named Thomas Veal, fearing the worst, hid out in the cave. Knowing that he could be turned over to authorities quite easily, Veal had a decision to make. Run? Or stay put. Well, he decided to stay put. Soon, he became a member of the community, working as a cobbler mending and making shoes. The residents of Lynn grew to accept Veal and welcomed him to stay.

Veal abandoned his pirating ways, but he also *never* strayed far from the treasure that he and his fellow pirates supposedly buried. Then, one day, while in the cave, tragedy struck. Whether from an explosion inside the cave or from a sudden earthquake that struck the land, a thunder roared across the cavern's opening. A moment later, Veal was gone — trapped behind, or possibly beneath, the rubble.

A member of the community had passed away, but his story lingered on. Many in Lynn had either deduced (or been told) that Veal was a pirate who had arrived that day on the shores to hide treasure. Over time, stories of Veal's treasure had been told and retold to countless local residents and, in the early 1830s, some of the residents decided to test the validity of the claim. Two attempts

were made to blast the cave and find the treasure, but both failed. Coincidence—or perhaps a pirate insuring that his treasure would be never found?

What happened next, however, is even more interesting then this classic New England pirate saga

The Mystery

In the mid 1800s, the rise of Spiritualism spread across America like a storm surge. The belief that people could communicate with spirits and talk with those who had migrated to the afterlife became a hobby with some and a fascination with others.

Hiram Marble was one man who was fascinated. He joined the Spiritualist Church in Charlton, Massachusetts and became dedicated to proving that the afterlife existed and that people could communicate with the dead.

One night in 1852, Hiram had a vision. The ghost of Thomas Veal, Marble claimed, came to him with a message. He spoke about a hidden treasure and explained that it was his for the taking.

"If you dig at Dungeon Rock," Veal's ghost allegedly claimed, "you will leave a rich man."

The vision excited Marble. He wasn't necessarily excited about the money, though that might have inspired him a bit. Rather, he was flabbergasted to have spoken to a ghost and wanted to prove that ghosts could indeed send reliable messages.

Marble quickly moved to Lynn and purchased Dungeon Rock and the land around it from the town. He set up a two-story house near the base of the rock and quickly moved his family to the location. Soon Hiram and his son Edwin began toiling at the rock, trying to prove that the treasure existed and that Hiram had indeed spoken to a ghost.

Hiram labored on the rock endlessly. Using picks and dynamite, the Marbles dug and dug. With his son, Hiram was able to clear about a foot of rock a month, constantly clearing the remaining rubble and placing it on the surrounding landscape.

Hiram continued his conversations with Veal, as well as Captain Harris, who occasionally offered his two bits about the location of the treasure. However, as Marble toiled on, his own personal funds eventually ran out—but fascination had turned to obsession. Hiram HAD to find the treasure! So, he began holding an early type of fundraiser, offering tours of the site to visitors to finance his project. Along with this, he held séances at night, sometimes communicating with the deceased to determine the location of the treasure. Eventually, the cave became a winding tunnel, based on the ruminations the ghosts shared with the mediums — who, in turn, shared it with Hiram — about the location of the treasure.

Hiram dedicated the remaining years of his life to the pursuit of the treasure and proof of the afterlife. When he died in 1868, Edwin took over, continuing his father's pursuit until his own death in 1880. Edwin asked to be buried at the site, where he remains to this day.

The treasure was never found. Whether or not it even exists remains unknown. Yet, the treasure seemed of a secondary nature to Hiram, as it's believed that he hoped to use the funds to purchase land for people of Lynn to enjoy as a public space.

As fate would have it, Hiram's wish came true. The land around Dungeon Rock was eventually given to the city of Lynn and opened for — you guessed right — a public park that people can enjoy.

Dungeon Rock remains open to the public to this day. No one can dig for treasure there, as Hiram once did, but they can revel in the amazing wealth of memories that still abound on the site. If you look closely, you will see the old foundation of the Marble house and find remnants of the Marbles' garden. You might even see Edwin's grave, which is marked by a pink rock at the top of a staircase that came out of the old family cellar.

However, you might just find a little bit more as well. For careful visitors to the site sense things, much like Hiram did way back when: a *feeling*...a *sense* of someone looking...strange lights...and shadows... all suggestions that the spirits that led Hiram to the spot might never have left. According to some people, spirits still visit Dungeon Rock to this day and perhaps even the Marbles themselves have paid the place a visit, attempting to prove what Hiram so long hoped to show — that people could talk in the afterlife.

Dungeon Rock still stands as a testimony to the hard work of Hiram Marble. And, in its shadow, might rest the realization of Marble's dreams...even if there is no buried treasure.

Part Ten:
Haverhill

*H*averhill was founded in 1640. Originally known as the Pentucket settlement, its founders were ten men from Ipswich and Newbury. They named the settlement for the Native American tribe in the area, but by 1642 they had purchased the land from the Native Americans. The men renamed the village Haverhill, after a town in England.

The town grew steadily as a farming village. In 1697, Haverhill was the site of a legendary Native American attack in which several town members were kidnapped or killed. Among them was Hannah Dunston, who was taken to New Hampshire. Once there, she turned on her captors, killed them, and returned safely to the village.

In the eighteenth century, Haverhill became known for its shipbuilding and cattle businesses. Its industry expanded, in the 1800s, to include a large shoe industry. In time, Haverhill became one of the shoe capitals of the world, and since then, the town has been home to many intriguing figures. These include the poet John Greenleaf Whittier, who was born in the town; John Macy, of Macy's fame, owned a store in town in the mid 1800s; and Louis Meyer, later of MGM fame, owned a theater in town in the early 1900s.

Haverhill has been known for a quiet history, which explains why it might also have a secret history all its own.

Is It or Isn't It...

Kimball Tavern

The building, located on Kim Street, used to be a tavern before becoming part of the now closed Bradford College. The tavern, as of this publication, was up for auction. But here's the tale of its possible haunting...

The History

*I*n 1690, the current city of Haverhill was at the nexus of travel routes in New England. Because of its central location between Boston and towns that are now in current day Maine, a small, quaint tavern was built in an ideal location. Called the Kimball Tavern, it served as an establishment for visitors from Boston and Maine. People could stop at the tavern, share a meal, and engage in local gossip.

The tavern was an important part of local affairs for more than three centuries. In 1803, a group of thirty visitors met in the tavern and decided that the area was in need of a school. From this humble beginning, Bradford Academy, an all-women's college, was formed in 1932. Over time, Kimball Tavern was purchased as one of the buildings for this college.

The tavern served many purposes, but as part of the college, it was used mainly as an academic building. Students often met in the former bar for discussions or presentations. Although Bradford College became a co-ed facility in 1971, enrollment declined during the next twenty-nine years. When Bradford College closed in 2000, the buildings were slowly sold off, with Kimball Tavern remaining in a state of transition, awaiting purchase.

The Mystery

While the Bradford College tradition may be relegated to history books and ardent memories of a strong alumni group, there are still a few skeletons that lurk in the closets of the former college. According to some alumni, Kimball Tavern, which has changed little in its three centuries of existence, might be home to a few ghosts.

An article in *The Eagle-Tribune,* a local newspaper in the North Shore region, says that several alumni have claimed that ghosts inhabit the former Haverhill meeting place—and they believe the spirits have lurked in the tavern for some time. They described their college days spent in the building—*where spirits watched over them*—and having presentations temporarily interrupted by faulty switches and suddenly unplugged equipment. The ghosts never seemed to bother anyone and simply appeared to be some type of *being* looking over the people who were in the classrooms.

The exact nature of these ghosts is unknown. Whether they are spirits of visitors from long ago or just the simple quirkiness of a building that is three hundred years old remains to be determined. However, in 2007, an apparent lead in the ghost theory appeared when people passing the tavern reported seeing eerie glowing lights in the building.

The mysterious nature of the lights intrigued the owners of the building as well as local history buffs. A small investigation was launched and soon it was discovered that the lights themselves are not that of an unearthly visitor. It appears that a rather touchy alarm system with blinking lights caused the eerie glow.

However, such evidence hardly sways the ardent alumni of Bradford College. Many believe the school was — and the tavern still is — haunted. After all, people visited the establishment for more than three hundred years…surely that might give fodder for at least one good ghost story.

Whether or not anything unusual is ever found in the building is a matter that will have to wait for new owners who one day have the honor of owning a little piece of history.

Part Eleven: Salisbury

*S*alisbury is a town in the extreme northeastern corner of Massachusetts that borders New Hampshire. Formed in 1638 as part of a settlement called Colchester, Salisbury was incorporated in 1640. During its early years, farms located near marshland and the ocean dominated the Salisbury settlement. As time progressed, Salisbury's proximity to the ocean and the Merrimack River became important. Residents began to make their money with ships in the region. By the 1800s, the advent of the railroad made Salisbury a major trade stop in New England. Yet, by the end of the century, the beachfront region of the town proved to be its greatest asset, as people began moving to the region, building houses, hotels, and cottages along the beach areas. Slowly, but surely, Salisbury developed into the major beach region that it is today. However, along with that, it has also developed the distinction of having one really good ghost story.

The Shipwrecked Ghosts...

The History

*S*alisbury Beach is a quaint New England getaway. Like many of the beaches on the North Shore, its cool waters and gentle sand make it a popular location during the long, hot summer days.

However, the popular beach was also the sight of a late nineteenth century tragedy. In April 1894, the Maine schooner *Jennie M. Carter* had left berth in Rockport, Maine and was making its way to New York with a cargo of stone and brick. As the ship meandered off the Ipswich shore, it encountered a sudden northeaster. Pounded by wind, rain, and waves, the schooner lost its main mast and rudder. Caught up in the mercy of the ocean, the ship was tossed about the ocean until coming to a rest offshore near Salisbury Beach.

Amid the rough waters, and weighted down by stones that forced the ship into the soft sand, the crew decided to abandon ship. They entered their lifeboats and lowered themselves into the waters whirling around the sandbar. Unfortunately, as they fled the floundering ship, their lifeboat capsized in the water and they perished in the sea. Lost in the escape were the ship's captain, his niece, and four crewmembers. Their bodies have never been seen again. If the crewmembers had remained on the ship — as was the case with the ship's cat — they in all likelihood, may have survived.

The ship eventually rested near the shore of the beach...long after the crew had abandoned it and disappeared into the murky darkness of the stormy night. The once proud vessel itself gave way to the Atlantic. As time and age took its toll on the hull of the ship, and shifting sands sank it deeper into the beach area, the remnants have slowly disappeared below the tides. However, at some points in the day, the ship's skeleton can still be seen—a cold reminder of the raw power of Atlantic storms—as remnants of the shipwreck can be found in the area of the present-day pizza shop and playground.

The Mystery

Although the crew of the ship may have disappeared from this life, there are some people who believe that their legacy permeates the shore long after they departed this world. Various people claim that Salisbury Beach is haunted, particularly near the site of the old shipwreck.

According to the stories, unusual lights have been seen floating near the surface of the old shipwreck, as well as near the beach area, reminiscent of ghostly orbs. Unusual noises have also been heard along the beach and near one of the buildings known as the Frolics building. On occasion, voices have been heard to echo in the area and across the beach, possibly calling through the sands of time to anyone who might listen.

Are these the ghosts of the long-lost crew of the ship? Perhaps. Or maybe they are just the strange sites and sounds of nature, issuing the ongoing cry of the ocean. Whatever the case, there's no doubt that Salisbury Beach has a strange story that just might continue to be told to this day.

Resources

The following is a list of the print, media, and Internet resources that were used to put together this collection of tales.

Salem Resources

"Baker's Island." *Welcome to Salem Massachusetts: The City Guide.* http://www.salemweb. com/tales/bakersisland.shtml.

Berger, Josef. *In Great Waters: The Story of the Portuguese Fishermen.* Manchester, New Hampshire: Ayer Publishing, 1980.

Brim, Angela. "The Ghost's of Haunted Salem." *The Scarlet Letter, Whispers from the Witch City of Salem, Massachusetts.* http://www.hauntedsalem.com/scarletletter/ issue_01/theghostsofhauntedsalem.html.

Cousins, Frank and Riley, Phil M. *The Colonial Architecture of Salem.* Minelola, New York: Courier Dover Press (now Dover Publications), 2000.

"Ghost Stories: The Curse of the *Charles Haskell.*" URL: http://members.rediff. com/1000jokes/mysteries/story.html.

Grave Addictions website. "The House of Seven Gables." http://www.graveaddiction. com/sevengab.html

"Here Lyeth Richard More." http://www.sail1620.org/discover_biography_here_ lyeth_richard_more.shtml

"His Death Recalls Ghost Ship." *The New York Times*, December 2, 1920. URL: http:// query.nytimes.com/gst/abstract.html?res=FB0911F6355411738DDDAB0894D A415B808EF1D3

House of Seven Gables website. URL: http://www.7gables.org

Jasper, Mark. *Haunted Inns of New England.* Yarmouthport, Massachusetts: On Cape Publications, 2000.

"Ropes Mansion." URL: http://www.graveaddiction.com/ropes.html

"Ropes Mansion." URL: http://www.salemmass.com/houses/buildings3.html.

"Salem Tales: Charter(ing) a Course through Times Past Charter Street." URL: http://www.salemweb.com/tales/charter.shtml.

"Salem Tales: Samuel McIntire." URL: http://www.salemweb.com/tales/mcintire. shtml.

"The Untold Story of 1692." *The Witch Dungeon Museum* website: http://www. witchhistorymuseum.com/witchhistory.html.

Toiles, Bryant Franklin Jr. et al. *Architecture in Salem: An Illustrated Guide.* UPNE: 2004.

Trask, Richard. *The Devil Hath Been Raised.* Danvers: Yeoman Press, 1997.

UFO Evidence: "July 16,1952- Salem, Massachusetts." URL: http://www.ufoevidence. org/photographs/section/1950s/Photo51.html.

Wagner, Stephen. "Ghosts of the Seven Gables." http://paranormal.about.com/od/ ghostphotos/a/aa100404.html.

"Welcome to the Ropes Mansion." URL: http://www.ropescorner.com/mansion1. html.

Danvers Resources

Boston's Haunted Places website: http://www.spiritsigns.org/Massachusetts%20 Haunted%20Places.html.

Danvers State Asylum website: http://www.danversstateinsaneasylum.com

"Ghosts in the Homestead." *The Nurse Homestead Newsletter*. Rebecca Nurse Homestead Preservation Society. URL: http://www.rebeccanurse.org/RNurse/ Homestead.html.

"Narrative History of the (Peabody Institute) Library." URL: http://www.danverslibrary. org/administration/pilhistlong2.html.

Puffer, Michael. "The lore, and lure, of Danvers State Hospital." *Danvers Herald*. October 29, 2003. URL: http://www.hauntedsalem.com/news/oct03-dh-danversstate.html.

Strange USA. Peabody Institute Library. URL: http://www.strangeusa.com/ viewlocation.aspx?locationid=4864.

"The Rebecca Nurse Homestead by Richard Trask." URL: http://www.rebeccanurse. org/RNurse/Homestead.html.

Website: Genealogy Forum File: Old Endicott Cemetery, Danvers, MA. http://www. genealogyforum.com/files/MA/EndicottCemeteryDanvers.html.

Beverly Resources

"About Endicott." Endicott College website: http://www.endicott.edu/servlet/Retriv ePage?site=endicott&page=AboutENHistory.html.

Bray, Matt. "History of the Cove." Primary Research website: http://www. primaryresearch.org/PRTHB/Neighborhoods/Cove/index.php

Cook, Sharon Love. "The Ghost of Winthrop Hall." *Supernatural Experiences*, ed. by Ginnie Siena-Bivona. Body, Mind, and Spirit, 2003.

"Endicott College: Historic Houses A Walking Tour." Endicott College website: http:// www.endicott.edu/walktour/index.html.

Haunted Places in Massachusetts website: http://www.shadowlands.net/places/ massachusetts.html.

Strange USA website: http://www.strangeusa.com/ViewLocation. aspx?locationid=4803

Marblehead Resources

"A Brief History of Marblehead." Marblehead, the Spirit of New England website: http://www.visitmarblehead.com/pages/history.asp

Burke, Allen. "Paranormal expert seeks Fort Sewall ghost." *Salem News*. August 6, 2008. URL: http://salemnews.com/punews/local_story_218235816.html.

Olson, Kris. "Does Fort Sewall hold spooky secrets?" Wicked Local Marblehead website: http:www.wickedlocal.com/marblehead/news/x81484727/Does-Fort-Sewall-hold-spooky-secrets

Gloucester Resources

Bill Franson photography – Dogstown. URL: http://www.bfranson.com/ billfransonphotg.html.

Babson Boulders website: http://www.capeannweb.com/babsonboulders.html.

"Ghosts of Massachusetts." Mysticalblaze website: http://www.mysticalblaze.com/ GhostsMassachusetts.html.

"Gloucesters Haunted Castle." The Cabinent.Com Dark Destinations website: http://www.thecabinet.com/darkdestinations/location.php?sub_id=dark_ destinations&location_id=hammond_castle

"Hammond Castle Museum Investigated." Associated Content website: http://www. associatedcontent.com/article/182898/hammond_castle_museum_investigation. html?image=67831&page=2&cat=16

MacDougall, Dan & Reed, Meredith. "Marblehead Monsters, the Truth About an Ancient Legend." *Marblehead Magazine*, summer 1981 (Vol. II, No. 1), with illustrations by Stephanie Hart McGrail.

O'Neill, J. P. "The Great New England Sea Serpent." 1999. URL: http://www.pibburns. com/tgness.html.

Sullivan, Paul. "Hammond Castle Setting for Mystery Novel." *Gloucester Daily Times*, November 26, 2007. URL: http://www.hammondcastle.org/common/index.ph p?com=HAMM&div=AA&nav=AA&page=A91

"The Gloucester Sea Serpent." The Museum of Hoaxes website: http://www. museumofhoaxes.com/serpent.html.

"Welcome to Hammond Castle Museum." Hammond Castle website: http://www. hammondcastle.org/common.

Essex Resources

"Gloucester History." Cape Ann Museum website: http://www.capeannhistoricalmuseum. org/history/gloucester_hist.html.

Grieco, Kristen. "Ghostly Galley: Strange things happen at Essex eatery." *Gloucester Daily Times*, October 29, 2007.

Newburyport Resources

"A Very Grave Matter." Gravestones & History of Newburyport, Essex Co., Massachusetts. URL: http://www.gravematter.com/cem-ma-newburyport5.asp.

Abell, L. G. *Gems by the Way-side*. New York, New York: R. T. Young, 1853.

Cardin, Sabrina. "Barmen say ghosts lurk in Brown Square Inn." *Daily News of Newburyport*. October 31, 2007. http://www.newburyportnews.com/punews/ local_story_304093943.

"Essex County sightings." The Gulf Coast Bigfoot Research Organization website: http://www.gcbro.com/MAessex0002.html

Friends of Parker River National Wildlife Refuge website: http://www.parkerriver. org/index.html.

"Garrison Inn." Garrison Inn website: http://www.garrisoninn.com/history.html.

Gems by the Wayside: An Offering of Purity and Truth – Google Books Result.

"Haunted Places in Massachusetts." Shadowlands website: http://theshadowlands. net/places/massachusetts.html.

"Haunted Schoolhouse of Newburyport." http://ghosts-hauntings.suite101.com/ article.cfm/haunted_schoolhouse_in_newburyport.

"Maudslay State Park." Department of Conservation and Recreation. URL: http:// www.mass.gov/dcr/parks/northeast/maud.htm

"Maudslay State Park." Shadowlands website: http://theshadowlands.net/ghost/ ghost263.html.

"Maudslay State Park." Wickipedia website: http://en.wikipedia.org/wiki/Maudslay_
State_Park.

New Plum Island Pages website: http://www.plum-island.com.

"Report 6631." The Bigfoot Field Researchers Organization website: http://www.
bfro.net/GDB/show_report.asp?id=6631.

"The Garrison Inn, Newburyport, MA." Massachusetts Paranormal Crossroads
website: http://www.masscrossroads.com/garrison.

The Haunted Schoolhouse at Newburyport, Mass. Boston, Massachusetts: Loring
Publishers, 1873. URL: http://www.letrs.indiana.edu/cgi/text/pageviewer-idx?
c=wright2;cc=wright2;sid=dd0695fe9eccc9c38c14a9bbcaaeb51a;idno=wrig
ht2-1128;view=image;seq=003.

"The Little Haunted Schoolhouse." http://www.masscrossroads.com/newschool.
html.

Nahant Resources

"Essex County Haunted Sites." URL: http://www.masscrossroads.com/essex.html.

"Ghosts of Boston, Massachusetts and Vicinity." URL: http://www.hollowhill.com/
ma/bos.html.

"Poetry and Places of Essex County: Egg Rock." URL: http://myweb.northshore.edu/
users/ccarlsen/poetry/lynn/egghistory.html.

"Strange New England: Swallow Cave." URL: http://www.strangene.com/wonders/
swallow.html.

Lynn Resources

About Lynn." City of Lynn website: http://www.ci.lynn.ma.us/about_lynn_history.
shtml.

D'Agostino, Thomas. *Pirate Ghosts and Phantom Ships.* Atglen, Pennsylvania: Schiffer
Publishing Ltd., 2008.

"Dungeon Rock." Friends of Lynn Woods website: http://www.flw.org/
dungeonrockhistory.html

Emerson, Nanette Snow. *The History of Dungeon Rock.* Boston, Massachusetts: B.
Marsh, 1869. URL: books.googlebooks.com

"Lynn History." Gordon College website: http://www.gorden.edu/page.cfm?iPageID
=655&iCategoryID=72&Gorden_In_Lynn&Lynn_History.

Haverhill Resources

Labella, Mike. "Where ghosts might stay, there's a mysterious light in the window." *The
Eagle-Tribune,* January 31, 2007. URL: http://www.eagletribune.com/punewshh/
local_story_031094553?keyword=topstory.

"Where is Haverhill, MA?" URL: http://www.haverhillusa.com/whereishaverhill.
html.

Salisbury Resources

"Gulf Log." *Gulf of Maine Times,* Summer, 2004. URL: http://www.gulfofmaine.org/
times/summer2004/gulflog.html.

"Salisbury Beach." Scary New England website: http://www.scarynewengland.com/
mastories.html.

Index